THE AWAKENING

A Novel of Beginnings

TWAYNE'S MASTERWORK SERIES

Robert Lecker, General Editor

THE AWAKENING

A Novel of Beginnings

Joyce Dyer

TWAYNE PUBLISHERS
An Imprint of Simon & Schuster Macmillan
NEW YORK

Prentice Hall International
LONDON · MEXICO CITY · NEW DELHI · SINGAPORE · SYDNEY · TORONTO

Twayne's Masterwork Studies No. 130

The Awakening: A Novel of Beginnings
Joyce Dyer

Twayne Publishers
An Imprint of Simon & Schuster Macmillan
1633 Broadway
New York, NY 10019-6785

Library of Congress Cataloging-in-Publication Data

Dyer, Joyce.
  The Awakening : a novel of beginnings / by Joyce Dyer.
    P. cm.—(Twayne's masterwork studies; no. 130)
  Includes bibliographical references (p.   ) and index.
  ISBN 0-8057-8382-2—ISBN 0-8057-8383-0 (pbk).
    1. Chopin, Kate, 1851–1904. Awakening. I. Title. II. Series.
PS1294.C63A64336   1993   93–4664
813'.4—dc20   CIP

The paper used in this publication meets the minimum requirements of American
National Standard for Information Sciences—Permanence of Paper for Printed Library
Materials. ANSI Z3948–1984. ∞

10 9 8 7 6 5 4 3 2 1 (hc)
10 9 8 7 6 5 4 3 2   (pb)

Printed in the United States of America

To Thomas and Annabelle

Contents

List of Illustrations

Note on the References and Acknowledgments

All references to *The Awakening* are taken from the Norton Critical Edition of the novel (New York: W. W. Norton & Company, 1976), edited by Margaret Culley.

Photographed material from the 1899 Herbert S. Stone & Company edition of *The Awakening* has been provided through the courtesy of the John M. Wing Foundation, Newberry Library, Chicago. The 1899 photograph of Chopin is included with the permission of the Stone and Kimball archives of the Newberry Library. Photographs of Esplanade Avenue and the Krantz Hotel have been reproduced with the agreement of the Historic New Orleans Collection in New Orleans, Louisiana.

Earlier versions of portions of chapters 6, 8, and 9 appeared in *Southern Studies, Markham Review, Southern Literary Journal*, and the MLA volume *Approaches to Teaching Chopin's "The Awakening"*. Grateful acknowledgment is made to *Markham Review* and *Southern Literary Journal* for granting permission.

Sydney Krause, Sanford Marovitz, and Ottavio Mark Casale deserve recognition and thanks for their enthusiastic support of my work on Chopin during the 1970s. I would also like to thank Pat Eldredge, Barbara Clements, Sandra Parker, David Anderson, John Shaw, Damaris Peters-Pike, George Gauthier, Gayle Uhler, Mildred Schwan, Eileen Manion, Jane McAvoy, Nancy Rosenberg, Vivian Makosky, James McClelland, Tom Davis, William Appling, Nora

Jones, Eric Gustavson, Lora Farnstrom, Andy Kmetz, Jerry Brodsky, and the Lake Erie Literary Society for their distinctive contributions to this project.

Tom Vince and the staff of the Hudson Public Library provided generous assistance throughout the preparation of this manuscript. The reference staffs of the Kent State University Library, the Cleveland Public Library, the Library of Congress, the Historic New Orleans Collection, and the Amstid Research Center have been extremely helpful. The Hiram College librarians Patricia Basu, Mary Lou Selander, Lisa Johnson, and Jeff Wanser, along with computer consultants Omer Prewett and Jeff Clark, have again and again amazed me with their resourcefulness, efficiency, and genuine concern for both scholarship and the people behind it.

I am deeply grateful to the hundreds of students at Lake Forest College, Western Reserve Academy, and Hiram College who have responded to *The Awakening* with affection and curiosity. They never let my mind rest. I am indebted to the National Endowment for the Humanities and *Reader's Digest* for granting me Ohio's Teacher-Scholar Award for 1990–91, allowing me to engage in reading and research complementary to this project. A Gerstacker-Gund summer grant from Hiram College, along with an award from the Paul E. Martin Faculty Endowment Fund, helped support the completion of this book.

There is, of course, no satisfactory way to thank Per Seyersted and Emily Toth for doing the difficult and essential work that has allowed Chopin scholarship to flourish.

My husband, Daniel, makes everything infinitely better than it would be otherwise—including this manuscript. Our son, Stephen, blesses us with his kindness and strength. Paul Steurer, Sr., Edith Steurer, Richard Dyer, Janice McCormick, Dave Dyer, Prudence Dyer, Edward Dyer, and Ronald Osborn all deserve my gratitude for their unfailing support and understanding.

Most of all, I lovingly acknowledge my father, Thomas W. Coyne, who died shortly before this book was completed, and my mother, Edna Annabelle Haberkost Coyne—my own dear Edna.

Kate Chopin, 1899
Courtesy of the Stone and Kimball archives, the Newberry Library, Chicago

Chronology:
Kate Chopin's Life and Work

1850   Catherine (Kate) O'Flaherty born in St. Louis on 8 February to
            Eliza Faris O'Flaherty and Captain Thomas O'Flaherty, a busi-
            nessman originally from Ireland.

1855   Enters St. Louis Academy of the Sacred Heart, where she
            forms an important friendship with Kitty Garesché, probably
            the model for the intelligent girlhood friend Edna Pontellier
            tells Adèle Ratignolle about. Thomas O'Flaherty, a founder of
            the Pacific Railroad, dies on the inaugural train when the
            Gasconade Bridge in Missouri collapses during a severe rain-
            storm.

1861   Confirmed in the Catholic Church by Archbishop Peter
            Richard Kenrick.

1863   Chopin's great-grandmother and influential teacher, Victoire
            Verdon Charleville, dies in January. Chopin later uses
            Madame Charleville's frank stories about St. Louis history and
            families in her fiction. One month later her adored half-broth-
            er George dies of typhoid fever while serving in the
            Confederate Army.

1867   Begins a commonplace book of poems, diary excerpts, essays,
            sketches, copied passages, and criticism.

1868   Graduates from Sacred Heart Academy.

1869–1870   Attends all the typical St. Louis debutante parties and functions
            but also learns to smoke and writes her first story,
            "Emancipation: A Life Fable," a short piece about freedom
            and constraint.

1870   Marries the Louisiana-born businessman Oscar Chopin in
            June. Keeps journal of European honeymoon. Moves to

Chronology

Magazine Street in New Orleans in October. In November Oscar's father, Dr. Victor Jean Baptiste Chopin, dies.

1871–1878 Bears five sons, Jean, Oscar Charles, George, Frederick, and Felix. Oscar Charles will be hired as a professional cartoonist by the *San Francisco Examiner* and his daughter Kate, named after his mother, will become a talented artist.

1879 Oscar closes his business in New Orleans, owing to poor cotton crops, and moves with his family to Cloutierville, where he manages several small plantations and buys a general store. Daughter Lélia is born.

1882 Oscar dies of malaria, leaving Kate with significant debt and six young children.

1883–1884 Attempts to run Oscar's businesses, an experience that provides the focus for her first novel, *At Fault*. Finally decides to move to St. Louis with her children to live with her mother.

1885 Eliza O'Flaherty dies very suddenly. Dr. Kolbenheyer, the model for Dr. Mandelet in *The Awakening*, begins to visit Chopin and to encourage her reading and writing.

1886 Moves to 3317 Morgan Street in St. Louis.

1888 Becomes acquainted with the work of Maupassant and is heavily influenced by his original brand of realism. Writes "Euphrasie," which is eventually revised and published by *Century* in 1894 as "A No-Account Creole."

1889 Her first publication, the poem "If It Might Be," appears in *America*. Writes four stories, including "A Point at Issue!" and "Wiser Than a God," all of which are published.

1890 Completes *At Fault* in April; after rejection by *Belford's Monthly* in Chicago, publishes 1,000 copies with Nixon-Jones Printing Company, St. Louis, at her own expense. Completes her second novel in November, *Young Dr. Gosse and Theo*, but destroys it several years later after ten rejections.

1890–1892 Becomes a member of the Wednesday Club, founded by Charlotte Stearns Eliot, the mother of T. S. Eliot, but resigns two years later. Satire of clubs and club women appears in several Chopin stories, and in *The Awakening* in the depiction of Mrs. Highcamp's daughter.

1891 Writes "Mrs. Mobry's Reason" and "A Shameful Affair," two thematically risky stories that are published by the *New Orleans Times-Democrat* in 1893. Successfully places numerous stories with *Youth's Companion* and *Harper's Young*

	People. Writes *An Embarrassing Position*, her only extant play.
1892	Continues to write short stories, including "At the 'Cadian Ball" (*Two Tales* [journal]) and "Désirée's Baby" (*Vogue*).
1893	On 4 May, the day of the Wall Street panic, Chopin travels to New York and Boston to seek publishers for *Young Dr. Gosse* and a short story collection. In October a hurricane destroys Grand Isle. Writes "At Chênière Caminada" (*New Orleans Times-Democrat*), her first story with a Grand Isle setting.
1894–1896	Keeps a diary, "Impressions."
1894	Writes "A Respectable Woman" (*Vogue*) in January, introducing the character of Gouvernail, who reappears in "Athénaïse" and *The Awakening*. Houghton Mifflin publishes *Bayou Folk* in March, giving Chopin national exposure as a short story writer. Composes "The Story of an Hour" (*Vogue*) in April. Attends a conference of the Western Association of Writers in Indiana in June, an experience that inspires her to publish "The Western Association of Writers" (*The Critic*), her attack on conventional and sentimental art.
1895	Houghton Mifflin rejects Chopin's idea for a translation of six "Mad Stories" by Maupassant. Writes several key stories about the mysterious inner life, including "Athénaïse" (*Atlantic*), "Two Portraits" (*Rankin*, 1932), "Fedora" (*Criterion*), and "Vagabonds" (*Rankin*, 1932).
1896	Writes three stories that will be published in *Vogue*, "The Recovery," "A Pair of Silk Stockings," and "The Blind Man." Writes "A Vocation and a Voice" (*St. Louis Mirror*).
1897	Publishes six essays under the title "As You Like It" for *Criterion*. *A Night in Acadie*, a second volume of short stories, is published by Way & Williams of Chicago.
1897–1898	Writes *The Awakening*.
1898	Transfers publishing rights for books from Way & Williams to Herbert S. Stone & Company. Writes "The Storm," which would not be published until 1969 (in *The Complete Works of Kate Chopin*, edited by Per Seyersted).
1899	*The Awakening* published by Herbert S. Stone & Company on 22 April.
1900	Herbert S. Stone & Company reverses its earlier decision to publish *A Vocation and a Voice*, Chopin's third collection of short stories. (It would not be published until Emily Toth's edition for Penguin in 1991.) Writes four stories, only one of which, "The White Eagle," is published (*Vogue*).

Chronology

1901   Writes and publishes only one story, "The Wood-Choppers" (*Youth's Companion*).

1902   Publishes her last story, "Polly" (*Youth's Companion*), a sentimental and undistinguished piece. Coincidentally, a story by emerging American realist Jack London ("The 'Fuzziness' of Hoockla-Heen") ends on the page where "Polly" begins. In a letter postmarked 4 February, Chopin invites her sister-in-law Marie Breazeale to the St. Louis World's Fair, but explains that the fair will probably not open on schedule.

1903   Moves to 4232 McPherson Avenue, a modest brick house in St. Louis.

1904   Suffers a cerebral hemorrhage at the St. Louis World's Fair on 20 August and dies two days later. Her simple granite gravestone bears only her name and dates of birth and death.

The Awakening

By

KATE CHOPIN

Author of "A NIGHT IN ACADIE,"
"BAYOU FOLKS," *Etc.*

HERBERT S. STONE & COMPANY
CHICAGO & NEW YORK
MDCCCXCIX

Title page of 1899 Herbert S. Stone & Company edition of *The Awakening*
Courtesy of the John M. Wing Foundation, the Newberry Library, Chicago

LITERARY AND
HISTORICAL CONTEXT

1

Background to the Novel

The last event Kate Chopin attended in her life was the St. Louis World's Fair. Planned to commemorate the centennial of the Louisiana Purchase (it was also known as the Louisiana Purchase Exposition), the fair opened a year late on 30 April 1904. During the 187 weekdays the fair remained open, the average daily attendance was 100,217.[1] Kate Chopin, a season subscriber, was often among those daily crowds. The last time Chopin attended the fair—on 20 August, an extremely hot day—she suffered a brain hemorrhage that ushered her into unconsciousness and ended her life two days later.

The fair, as Chopin may well have sensed, was a perfect symbol of the period during which she wrote. Temporary "palaces" were erected out of papier-mâché and fiber to introduce fair-goers to the miraculous changes that were occurring in science and technology—the Palace of Electricity, the Palace of Agriculture, the Palace of Varied Industries, the Palace of Transportation. *Advance Souvenir*—an illustrated souvenir booklet that sold for 25 cents—lured visitors with the promise of a giant 8,000-horsepower turbine, "wireless telegraphy," stylish automobiles, airships, dairy innovations, the spectacular Cascade Gardens, and "apparatus for the electro-chemical industries."[2] The fair celebrated progress and the present.

But, paradoxically, the fair also celebrated the past, the old, conservative ways and symbols that were quiet and reassuring in restless times. The architecture of the palaces that housed engines and electric inventions—triumphal arches, Ionic pillars, towers, domes, and sculptures of heroic gods and goddesses—reflected past times. A 56-foot statue of Vulcan, weighing over 100,000 pounds, was placed in the center of the Palace of Mines and Metallurgy; Festival Hall featured a sculpture of Apollo and the Muses.[3] John Wesley Hanson, an exuberant supporter and historian of the fair, called the palaces, collectively, "an immaculate array of structures that carries the spectator back to the days of Greek and Roman splendor."[4] Even the buildings that housed the exhibits of individual states were frequently historic replications. The Louisiana state building, for example, was styled after the Cabildo, a government building in the French Quarter where France transferred the Louisiana territory to the United States in 1803 (*Advance Souvenir*, 19).

The mile-long Street of Amusements, known to visitors as the "Pike," most vividly represented the incongruity of the times. An exhibit called "Under and Over the Sea" created the illusion for fair visitors of going by submarine to Paris and returning by airship. But on the same street, the Story of Creation was depicted, with a voice reading Scripture resounding in the background; Ancient Rome could be revisited, complete with chariots and horses; and the Faustian Hereafter ("A Gruesome Show") could be entered through the Cave of the Dead (Hanson, 123–28).

We do not know, of course, how Kate Chopin spent her time wandering the 1,240 acres of fairgrounds during the spring and summer of 1904. But might she have been attracted to the often grotesque tension the fair represented? We know that Henry Adams was. Toward the end of *The Education of Henry Adams* (1907), he mockingly describes the fair as "a pageant as ephemeral as a stage flat." He continues: "One asked oneself whether this extravagance reflected the past or imaged the future; whether it was a creation of the old American or a promise of the new one."[5]

This tension between the old and the new, between the nineteenth century and the twentieth, the traditional and the modern, always fascinated and challenged Chopin, and she wrote about it in story after story, including *The Awakening.*

The 1890s were very complicated years; changes occurred in that decade that would permanently alter life as nineteenth-century Americans had known it. The works of Darwin, Spencer, and Huxley were transforming intellectual thought. Chopin's friend and contemporary William Schuyler first noted the influence of such thinkers on Chopin.[6] Per Seyersted, who wrote a 1969 biography of Chopin, feels that her reading of science "confirmed her in her belief of the relativity of morals," a theme that certainly surfaces in the behavior of Edna Pontellier.[7] Fixed truth in any form—moral or religious or scientific—seldom escaped Chopin's ironic glance.

In *The Awakening*, of course, it was the fixed idea of women's roles that most concerned Chopin. She and other women were beginning to set down the roots of modern feminism during the 1890s. As the historian Mary Ryan has noted, five million women would join the work force by 1900.[8]

A few strong women were demonstrating new independence in their daily lives. Martha Louise Munger Black left her husband because he would not undertake an adventure to the Klondike in 1898: "I wrote to Will that I had made up my mind to go to the Klondyke [sic] as originally planned, that I would never go back to him, so undependable he had proven, that I never wanted to hear from or see him again. He went his way. I went mine."[9] Charmian Kittredge (who married Jack London in 1905) occasionally shocked East Bay society by "her daring rides astride alone in the hills and her familiarity with writers thought to be of questionable morals such as Thomas Hardy and Henrik Ibsen."[10]

Elizabeth Cady Stanton saw her radical work, *The Woman's Bible*, published in 1895—two weeks after her eightieth birthday.[11] Susan B. Anthony, who turned seventy in 1890, campaigned throughout the decade for the enfranchisement of women. Her biographer, Kathleen Barry, writes, "Between January and July of 1895 she had been to Atlanta, Georgia, had toured through Kentucky, Tennessee, and Louisiana, then had returned to Washington, D. C., and finally home to Rochester" (308). In a 17 October 1900 inscription to a book (her own biography, written by Ida Husted Harper), which she presented to Thomas Dickinson Boyles and Rachel Yates on the occasion of their wedding, Anthony articulated the views she shared with Lucretia Mott about the new terms of "ideal" marriages: "Would you be truly happy, you should in the language of the sainted *Lucretia Mott*, Let your *Dependence* be *mutual*, Your *Independence, equal*, Your *Obligations, reciprocal.*"[12] Frances Dickinson, Anthony's first cousin, would graduate in 1883 from the Women's Medical College of Chicago, become the first woman admitted to membership in the International Medical Congress, join the Chicago Woman's Club and Woman's Federated Labor Union, No. 2703—and, according to the recollection of family, learn to fly planes.[13]

In 1898 Charlotte Perkins Gilman, who was, like Anthony, a member of the National American Woman Suffrage Association (Barry, 310), published *Women and Economics*, which advocates women becoming more economically independent, thereby improving their marriages and increasing their own humanity. Gilman felt, as Chopin did, that relationships founded on economic dependence and expectations about the performance of household duties needed to be reexamined. She wrote: "Marriage is not perfect unless it is between class equals. There is no equality in class between those who do their share in the world's work in the largest, newest, highest ways and those who do theirs in the smallest, oldest, lowest ways."[14]

Other writers of the 1890s besides Chopin questioned women's traditional roles. As Larzer Ziff points out in *The American 1890s* (1966), "To be a serious female author in the nineties was to be a writer of stories about women and their demands."[15] Authors like Ellen Glasgow and Theodore Dreiser were looking at the effects of urban living on relationships between men and women, sometimes exploring issues Gilman, too, thought significant. Sarah Orne Jewett was writing about strong friendships between her courageous and honest New England women, not about conventional romances.

Women in the 1890s, however, including women writers, could be only so bold. Popular culture reflected the nation's suspicion of women who chose untraditional roles. The typewriter, for example, came to represent the evil influence of office work on America's once-domestic women. Thomas Getz in 1889 composed the popular song, "Since My Daughter Plays on the Typewriter," in which an Irish father mourns the changes his daughter, Bridget Maguire, has undergone since becoming a typist. She is rude to her mother—"high-ton'd"—flirtatious with her boss, and forgetful of her Irish upbringing. In the last verse the father proclaims,

> Sure she's gone to the devil entirely,
> She's bleach'd her hair till it is lighter
> And I'll dance a Can-Can on the face of the man,
> That taught her to play the Typewriter.[16]

The historians Linda Kerber and Jane S. DeHart explain that even as women were becoming increasingly political in the nineteenth century, increasingly more public, they were doing so almost always under the guise of "Motherhood"—at first, "Republican Motherhood," and later, "Reformist Motherhood" and "Political Motherhood."[17] One such woman was Mary Harris Jones, the powerful, courageous, and dangerous labor activist of the nineteenth and early twentieth centuries who was named official organizer for the United Mine Workers (UMW) by the president, John Ratchford, in 1897: in spite of her radical ideology, she insisted on being called "Mother Jones" and always dressed like a Victorian grandmother in black bombazine with a fancy black hat and a lace jabot.

The great majority of novels with "subversive" themes nevertheless had acceptable resolutions. Even before the 1890s, a large group of women writers—dubbed the "literary domestics" by the historian Mary Kelley—were focusing on female experience, though largely as defined by the domestic sphere.[18] Ziff, discussing novels of the 1890s, concludes that they often contain fairly strong statements about women's right to equality, but that most offer only timid resolutions. "The new theme of the independent woman called for a new plot that would not resistlessly flow to the magnetic terminal of marriage, but the young lady writers of the nineties dared enough when they dared the theme," he explains. "Their works are marred and sometimes destroyed because they cannot break free of the marriage pattern" (285).

Even the divorced woman—the new woman entering fiction from the mid-nineteenth century on—and the widow often found their salvation in remarriage. This was true for Thérèse Lafirme, the heroine of Chopin's first novel, *At Fault* (1890). Thérèse marries David Hosmer (of course, only after he is forced by Thérèse to attempt a reconciliation with his wife Fannie, who then conveniently dies) and rediscovers bliss. "Through love they had sought each other, and now the fulfillment of that love had brought more than tenfold its promise to both. It was a royal love; a generous love and a rich one in its revelation. It was a magician that had touched life for them and changed it into a glory."[19]

Some single women—or divorced women—in nineteenth-century novels do refuse to marry, or remarry. These women either withdraw from society, like Marcia Hubbard in William Dean Howells's *Modern Instance* (1881), or commit themselves to a righteous cause. In Mary Noailles Murfree's mountain novel, *The Prophet of the Great Smoky Mountains* (1885), Dorinda Cayce audaciously refuses to marry Rick Tyler after he fails to testify on behalf of an innocent man. As Dorinda makes her announcement, she simultaneously pledges herself to the care of Aunt Jerushy's baby. Marcia Hubbard, though considered eccentric by the village, lives an "unmolested life."[20] And Dorinda remains supremely virginal—and therefore supremely acceptable to nineteenth-century readers.

Female passion was thought to be immoral and unhealthy by even some of the most aggressive proponents of realism and feminism in the last decades of the nineteenth century. To suggest otherwise was to enter extremely perilous waters, the waters in which Edna herself swims. Consequently, female characters who were separated from men—by their unmarried status, their disillusionment with husbands, or divorce—seldom considered the avenue of liberated sexual behavior an option.

The 1890s was the decade, we must remember, when audiences were scandalized by the first long embrace on the screen in *The John Rice-May Irwin Kiss*. R. W. Gilder, the editor of *Century*—one of the most important literary magazines of the decade, it published Twain, Howells, Chopin, London, and Wharton—frequently encouraged his authors to make their stories more pleasing (that is, more morally wholesome and sweet). Although Howells created the famous image of a real rather than ideal grasshopper to register his preference for what is true, he was careful to provide his own definition of realistic truth.[21] Howells admired American novelists who avoided writing books like *Anna Karenina* (1873) and *Madame Bovary* (1857). Such books, Howells thought, were "cheap and meretricious" and lacked fidelity to "feeling and character" because they focus so heavily on just one passion rather than on the many that exist—on just "the passion of guilty love" (1891, 156–57).

Even Charlotte Perkins Gilman, one of the most radical voices of the decade, spoke out strongly against female eroticism. We might guess that the far more enthusiastic reception of Gilman's text over Chopin's was related to Gilman's conservative position on sexual issues. For Gilman, sex was useful for reproduction only; what she called "excessive sex-indulgence" (caused in her opinion by abnormal "sex-distinction") functioned only "to pervert and exhaust desire as well as to injure reproduction" (30–31). Gilman defended the sanctity of marriage (however radically modified a form of it), along with the sanctity of monogamy and fidelity. Life's greatest evil, Gilman claimed, consisted of "promiscuous and temporary sex-relations" (94).

In a decade that made Charles M. Sheldon's *In His Steps: "What Would Jesus Do?"* (1896) one of its most popular books, it was not surprising to hear frequent warnings about sex also coming from the country's pulpits. Thomas DeWitt Talmage, one of the most influential and severe pulpit speakers of his day, shouted out the dangers of immoral literature—of books that made "impurity decent." And what should good Christians do who find themselves in possession of such unprincipled volumes? "Kindle a fire on your kitchen hearth," he advised, "or in your back yard, and then drop the poison in it, and keep stirring the blaze until from preface to appendix there shall not be a single paragraph left, and the bonfire in your city shall be as consuming as that one in the streets of Ephesus."[22] Thus were the early beginnings of feminism in America linked with eternal damnation.

Physicians, too, were generally using their authority to prescribe conventional behavior as well as medicine. Dr. Mandelet is far more understanding, far more advanced in his knowledge of female sexual psychology, than the majority of the decade's physicians. Some doctors, such as Gilman's physician, S. Weir Mitchell, and Professor Ward Hutchinson, emphatically insisted on the curative value of domesticity. The anatomy and temperament of women were seen as perfectly suited to motherhood; thus, equilibrium and health could be gained only through its pursuit. Nervous maladies, often growing out of severe sexual and domestic unhappiness, were lumped under the label "neurasthenia" by the period's physicians. Ryan notes, "Legions of physicians designed cures and built sanitariums for its treatment" (224). The growing discontent with orthodox physicians and their treatment of women's "complaints" and diseases revealed itself in the tremendous popularity of Lydia E. Pinkham's Vegetable Compound, a sort of nineteenth-century Geritol. The Lydia E. Pinkham Medicine Company, launched in 1875, made a profit of $1,185,847 in 1913 and enjoyed its peak year in 1925.[23]

To have a full sense of the shock Edna's behavior causes other characters in the novel—and caused Chopin's own reviewers—we need to remember that New Orleans, where much of *The Awakening* is set, had a triple history: it was, of course, American in many senses, but it was also southern and Creole. New Orleans felt the energy and changes of the nation. Margaret Culley notes that the 1890s brought hints of the women's movement to the Crescent City. Susan B. Anthony, for example, visited New Orleans in 1895. Women were entering new professions, becoming barbers, undertakers, cigar importers, insurance agents, and liquor dealers.[24]

Nevertheless, Louisiana remained an extremely conservative state. In 1808 Louisiana adopted the *Digest of the Civil Laws Now in Force in the Territory of Orleans*, patterned on the *Code Napoleon* of France. The Louisiana Code, which firmly established the husband as the head of the family, was still determining the conditions of marriage contracts at the end of the century. According to article 1388 of the code, the patriarchal structure of the Louisiana family was not a negotiable matter. And in article 1124 married women, along with babies and the mentally deranged, were declared incompetent to make contracts.[25]

Marie Fletcher, describing the depiction of Louisiana women in local color fiction, writes, "Basically they have much in common with the genteel ladies of the past, for they still represent the ideal of the fragile and lovely girl who is pure of character."[26] In their report to the Louisiana Purchase Exposition Commission in 1905, the Board of Lady Managers, chaired by Mary Margaretta Manning, continued to take its greatest pride in the creation of a social center on the exposition grounds, "their province being that of *National* Hostesses,—their privilege to extend a generous and far-reaching hospitality to all official dignitaries from home and abroad who visited the Exposition."[27] They were not, like Edna, questioning the importance of such afternoon receptions.

The Creole women of Louisiana, though seemingly less constrained than other women, were actually among the most conservative members of their sex in the nineteenth century. Like Adèle, they were frank and physical. But it was their unquestionable personal and religious commitment to family, chastity, husband, and children that made this open manner possible. For them, Mary Shaffter wrote in 1892, "women's rights . . . are the right to love and be loved, and to name the babies rather than the next president or city officials."[28] Edna, not a Catholic but a Presbyterian, not a Creole but a southerner, adopts the candor and sensual manner of her Creole friends yet leaves their traditional notions of wifehood and motherhood behind.

The tensions between the old and the new, the traditional and the untraditional, were great during the final years of the nineteenth century. It is not surprising that a country faced with such difficult and complex questions would sometimes turn to sentiment and easy answers for escape. Americans of the 1890s adored Reginald DeKoven's light opera *Robin Hood* (1890) (which ran for 3,000 performances), Joel Chandler Harris's *Nights with Uncle Remus* (1892), Margaret M. Saunders's classic dog tale, *Beautiful Joe* (1894), and John Philip Sousa's "The Stars and Stripes Forever" (1896). The year

1900 would see the publication of L. Frank Baum's *The Wonderful Wizard of Oz* (adapted for the stage in 1901) and Beatrix Potter's *The Tale of Peter Rabbit*.

The St. Louis World's Fair, with its displays and exhibits of both the old and the new, was the perfect event to bridge two centuries. Chopin lived during that transitional time. Her work offers the promise of new beginnings, but never the false promise that it will be easy. It is sadly appropriate that Chopin died after a day at the fair—literally and metaphorically, her fascination with the tension the fair displayed had a hand in killing her. Both as a visitor to the fair and as a writer she risked security and safety in the pursuit of change and exploration. Boldness drove Chopin to the fairgrounds on a day when the sun was too severe. Boldness also led her to compose *The Awakening* at the wrong time: when reviewers were ready for neither the questions she asked nor the study of females in transition that she eloquently and painfully undertook.

2

The Importance of the Work

Kate Chopin's *The Awakening* is unique in the canon of late nineteenth-century American literature. Ironically, some aspects of the novel's uniqueness caused early reviewers to greet it with hostility. Its uniqueness also led to its disappearance until the 1950s, when the French critic Cyrille Arnavon translated it and respected American critics such as Van Wyck Brooks, Robert Cantwell, and Kenneth Eble began writing about it. Published in 1899, significantly, it recorded with bold truth what one woman's attempt to join the twentieth century would entail, and it anticipated the journeys of the millions of other women, real and fictional, who would follow her.

Although it is mainly the unusual and complex character of Edna Pontellier and the novel's radical themes that have gained the attention of both readers and critics, the book's style also is noticeably original. Divided into 39 sections of strikingly different lengths, Chopin's 1899 volume represents a radical break not only from her conventionally arranged first novel, *At Fault* (1890), but also from most nineteenth-century American fiction. Poetic interludes are interspersed between more traditionally narrated segments; these provocative, lyrical, sometimes Whitmanesque sequences instruct us through our ears and senses

13

more strongly than through our intellects. Within each narrative segment there is often a powerful central symbol: an archetypal garden, a mythic moon, a Dionysian banquet, a romantic sea, strains of Frédéric Chopin and Richard Wagner. Kate Chopin has often been linked with turn-of-the-century realists and naturalists, Norris and Dreiser especially. Although there are components of both realism and naturalism in her style, Chopin also experiments with a very modern form of psychological symbolism in *The Awakening* that is absolutely her own.

The sexual candor of *The Awakening* was strikingly different from that of other novels written at the century's close. Chopin was certainly not the only writer of her time to use sexual language (nor, of course, was her language as explicit as we commonly find in novels today). Other writers included suggestive lines and phrases in their books. For example, in *McTeague*, a novel published the same year as *The Awakening*, Frank Norris describes his dentist as a "young bull in the heat of high summer" just before he kisses Trina "grossly, full on the mouth." We watch him fumble through Trina's closet, gathering her clothes greedily in his arms, "plunging his face deep among them, savoring their delicious odor with long breaths of luxury and supreme content."[1]

Seyersted, however, notes that realists and naturalists like Crane, Garland, Norris, and Dreiser—writers who were also exploring sexual force—seldom describe the passion of their female characters. "Their heroines—Maggie, Rose, Trina, and Carrie—are all rather sexless compared to Edna, and their descriptions of sexual matters in general are tame" (191). Although Chopin's sexual descriptions may seem mild to modern readers, contemporary readers would have found them inexcusably explicit. They were not accustomed to reading descriptions like these: "It was the first kiss of her life to which her nature had really responded. It was a flaming torch that kindled desire" (83); "His hand had strayed to her beautiful shoulders, and he could feel the response of her flesh to his touch" (92). As Barbara Solomon writes, "When we note that a year after the publication of *The Awakening*, Theodore Dreiser published *Sister Carrie*, which was considered so shocking and immoral that the copies of the novel were never delivered to the bookstores, we can gauge how revolutionary

The Importance of the Work

Kate Chopin's depiction of the force of Edna's passionate nature must have been. Dreiser excludes any scene of a sexual nature between Carrie and Drouet as she becomes his mistress."[2]

But it was not just Chopin's descriptions of sex that disturbed her contemporaries. Other elements in her presentation of sexuality were even more alarming. First, as we have mentioned, by writing about the passion of a woman, Chopin was automatically putting herself at great risk. Second, she was suggesting that guilt should not accompany sex, not even extramarital sex. After consummating her relationship with Alcée Arobin, Edna feels "neither shame nor remorse" (83). Third, Chopin refused to judge Edna as an immoral fallen woman, choosing instead a narrative voice that provides distance and ambiguity. Critics are still debating whether Edna is strong or weak, moral or immoral, responsible or irresponsible. Fourth, Chopin was making the bold assertion that perhaps a woman's sexual growth does not end with her marriage, a proposition that her own century would not tolerate. Indeed, as Ziff proposes, Chopin was ready "to treat [marriage] as yet another episode in the continuing development of feminine self-awareness, no more terminal than a birthday party" (285). And finally, Chopin was questioning whether sexuality and motherhood must be linked, as they certainly were in conventional Creole women like Adèle.

Unique, too, is Chopin's stress on the spiritual components of Edna's awakening and journey. That a woman might have both an active sexual life and an active spiritual life was incongruous to the nineteenth century. Yet Edna did. Briefly comparing Edna's attitude toward money with Trina's and Carrie's in *McTeague* (1899) and *Sister Carrie* (1900) establishes her spiritual superiority. All three women enjoy some degree of economic independence—the condition urged by Charlotte Perkins Gilman—but Edna shares neither Trina's obsession with money nor Carrie's understanding that it is linked to social ambition and success. Edna relies on the inheritance from her mother, as well as the money she makes from gambling at the races and her own painting, to purchase spiritual freedom. After she leaves her spacious "cottage" on Esplanade Street and begins to rent a small four-room "pigeon-house" around the corner, Edna experiences "a feeling of having descended in the social scale, with a corresponding sense of having risen in the spiritual" (93). Her own painting, and the music of her friend Mademoiselle Reisz, are far more valuable to her than the expensive possessions her husband chooses for the house, "the cut glass, the silver, the heavy damask" (50).

Edna's spiritual vision at times becomes deeply existential and uncannily modern, darkening the book yet making us feel even more that the story is ours. There are days, we are told, "when life appeared to her like a grotesque pandemonium and humanity like worms struggling blindly toward inevitable annihilation" (58). Darkness and death stand ominously in the wings of the novel, always looking on. Even Emma in Flaubert's *Madame Bovary* (1857) lacks the spiritual dimension of Edna, for Emma is completely consumed by dreams of aristocratic pleasure, of lovers dressed in lace and velvet. It is Edna Pontellier who seems the true ancestor of the twentieth-century woman.

Chopin refuses to shy away from the difficulties and complications of making the transition from one century to another, from the Victorian code of womanhood to a more modern version. The publication date of 1899 could not be more appropriate: it keeps Edna poised on the brink of the twentieth century but reminds us that she has not yet joined it. As modern as Edna seems at times, she has deeply absorbed many of the attitudes of her century and her culture and cannot step lightly or unencumbered into a new age.

Although Edna is no Emma Bovary, she, too, is overly susceptible to romance. For most of the novel, for example, Edna searches for definition and fulfillment through her impossible dreams of Robert Lebrun. She is also too susceptible to her age's attitude that women should adopt a casual, domestic attitude toward art and toward friendships. So although Edna is clearly creative, sensitive, responsive, and naturally able, as well as committed at times to the exploration and improvement of her talent ("I am becoming an artist. Think of it!" [63]), she lacks discipline, too often seeks a superficial social life rather than the solitary life, and looks for approval and friendship from casual artists like Adèle rather than from the true artist and potentially her true friend—Mademoiselle Reisz.

One final very important issue that Chopin does not allow Edna to avoid is that of motherhood. "A fact which significantly sets off *The Awakening* from *Maggie, Rose, McTeague,* and *Sister Carrie,*" Seyersted writes, "is that Edna has children and the other heroines do not" (192). Edna cannot reconcile her responsibility to her two young sons with her responsibility to herself. She chooses not to live in a world that forces her to value herself first as a mother and second as a human being. She is born into the new century too young to know how to change this equation. Chopin decides there will be no easy answers for Edna, just as there would be no easy answers for the women of the twentieth century who followed her.

In her own criticism of contemporary literature, Chopin found chiefly one criterion for labeling a book "immoral": "because it is not true."[3] This, of course, was not the criterion of Chopin's own reviewers; they repeatedly used the label "immoral" to describe *The Awakening,* even though truth was its single pursuit. The book's unique truthfulness about sex, spiritual discovery, and change—presented in a revolutionary style that ironically, was often applauded—led to the hostile early reviews that would be largely responsible for its disappearance for over half a century.

Yet now, in high schools and colleges throughout the nation, *The Awakening* is one of America's most frequently and successfully taught novels. Bernard Koloski, the editor of the Modern Language Association's *Approaches to Teaching Chopin's "The Awakening"* (1988), speaks about the academic popularity of the novel. "An MLA survey taken in preparation for this volume shows the novel being used in no fewer than twenty college courses—on subjects ranging from American literature, women's literature, and women's studies to realism, textual linguistics, folklore, and composition. At a time when some of America's important fiction has gone out of print, *The Awakening* was in 1987 available in at least eight paperback editions and was included in its entirety in three of the four major college anthologies of American literature and in the *Norton Anthology of Literature by Women.*"[4] It is highly ironic that the book's rare truthfulness, the very quality that almost buried it forever, has assured *The Awakening* a prominent and permanent place in American fiction.

3

Critical Reception

Having a group of people at my disposal, I thought it might be entertaining (to myself) to throw them together and see what would happen. I never dreamed of Mrs. Pontellier making such a mess of things and working out her own damnation as she did. If I had had the slightest intimation of such a thing I would have excluded her from the company. But when I found out what she was up to, the play was half over and it was then too late.

Kate Chopin, "Aims and Autographs of Authors" (1899)

Kate Chopin's tongue-in-cheek retraction of *The Awakening* indicates not only the amount of annoyance the book caused early critics but also their primary complaint: the character of Edna Pontellier.[1] The critics of 1899 were somewhat schizophrenic in their commentary. Almost without exception they admired Chopin's skill as a writer and her prose style, but also almost without exception they found her heroine a morally offensive woman.

Frances Porcher, who reviewed Chopin's novel for the *St. Louis Mirror*, typified that schizophrenia. Porcher praised the book's beauty of description and style but cringed at Edna's passion, calling it "an ugly, cruel, loathsome monster." She concludes: "There is no fault to find with the telling of the story, there are no blemishes in its art, but it leaves one sick of human nature and so one feels—*cui bono!*"[2] Literary prudishness, often the cause of schizophrenic commentary, was registered by critics for the *Chicago Times-Herald*, *Public Opinion*, the *Nation*, and *Literature*. Edna was described repeatedly as a shameful woman and an unacceptable focus for a book.

Until Emily Toth actually checked the holdings of the St. Louis Mercantile Library in preparation for her 1990 biography, the story prevailed that *The Awakening* had been banned from the library's shelves in response to negative and damning reviews like these. Toth shows that what she considers the "legend" of the banning began with an unsupported remark of Daniel Rankin, with the 1949 comments of Chopin's son Felix to Charles van Ravenswaay, and with a story told by a former librarian at the Mercantile Library to Per Seyersted in the 1960s. Records indicate that the Mercantile bought four copies of Chopin's *The Awakening* between 29 April and 28 June of 1899. Toth is not troubled by the designation "condemned" beside entries for the book in the library's records, noting that the term meant "de-accessioned," and that the books were more than likely worn out. Also, the notation could have been made anytime between 1899 and 1959, when the library converted to a different cataloging system.[3] Although Toth's new research is significant and convincing, it remains clear that negative reviews nonetheless had an adverse effect on the book's distribution and popularity. It was reprinted in 1906 by Duffield, but quickly went out of print again.

Although Chopin never voiced her response to her novel's reception except indirectly, it has been generally assumed that she lost confidence.[4] During the 1949 interview with Charles van Ravenswaay, Chopin's son Felix said, "Her second novel, however, created a furor which hurt her deeply. . . . She was broken hearted at the reaction to the book."[5] She did continue to write, and to publish, after 1899, even though many of her very late stories were highly conventional, with sentimental resolutions. Although we may wish she had written more stories like "The White Eagle" and "A Vocation and a Voice" during the last years of her life, such pieces do offer evidence that her spirit was not completely deadened by the harsh and unsympathetic response of early critics.

In the 25 years after her death Chopin's name was included in several reference works on Louisiana and the South. Writers of these reference entries built the case, however, that Chopin's stories about the Cane River region were her major achievement—not her novel. For example, the critics Leonidas Rutledge Whipple (*Library of Southern Literature* [1907]) and Fred Lewis Pattee (*A History of American Literature since 1870* [1915]) registered their clear preference for Chopin's short fiction. Perhaps this should not be surprising since the title pages of both the Stone and Duffield editions of *The Awakening* identify Kate Chopin as the "Author of 'A Night in Acadie,' 'Bayou Folks,' Etc."

Critical schizophrenia about *The Awakening* resurfaced in the 1930s, strengthened, at times, by the new emphasis on Chopin's short fiction. Daniel Rankin, her first biographer, registered his preference in 1932 for Chopin's short fiction. He noted the "exquisite care" of her writing, but he also found the novel "exotic in setting, morbid in theme, erotic in motivation."[6] Arthur Hobson Quinn praised the book in 1936 for its striking reality and "admirable economy" but nevertheless labeled Edna "selfish" and called the book a study of "morbid psychology." Like Pattee and others before him, Quinn reserved his highest praise for Chopin's "Désirée's Baby," calling it "one of the greatest short stories in the language."[7]

In the 1940s *The Awakening* almost vanished from American letters. Carlos Baker's entry on Chopin for Robert Spiller's 1948 edition of *Literary History of the United States* reflected no awareness of Chopin's 1899 novel, although Baker did refer to the first novel, which appeared in 1890. Baker admired Chopin's "intensity, courage, vigor, and independence" but focused his discussion exclusively on her short stories. The one fortunate service he did provide, however, was to question the perfection of "Désirée's Baby." Baker found the trick ending damaging and marring rather than ingenious.[8] Also, Chopin's name did not appear in the "Individual Authors" section of Spiller's 1948 bibliography—although writers like Mary Noailles Murfree did—nor was it included in the 1959 bibliography supplement. Joseph

Critical Reception

Reilly wrote an extremely affectionate and admiring essay about Chopin in his volume *Of Books and Men* (1942). He proposed that a dozen stories compiled from Chopin's two collections of short fiction would create a single work "which those most proud of American literature would gladly proclaim an addition to its masterpieces."[9] The great irony of his lengthy and devoted piece, however, is that Reilly, apparently unaware of its existence, never mentions *The Awakening*.

Not an American but a French critic was largely responsible for the revival of *The Awakening*. In 1946 Cyrille Arnavon wrote an article about Chopin's novel for *Romanciers américains contemporains*, and in 1953 he published a translation of *The Awakening* (retitling it *Edna*) with an elaborate introduction. In that introduction Arnavon qualified his praise of the novel but nonetheless established its importance and permanent value. He found Edna regressive and the suicide largely unjustified, but, nonetheless, he claimed the work was an American *Madame Bovary* ("cette *Bovary américaine*"[10])—a parallel first drawn by Willa Cather in her 1899 review of the novel for the *Pittsburgh Leader*.[11]

American critics of the 1950s finally began to recognize how deserving *The Awakening* was of serious attention. In *The Confident Years: 1885–1915* (1952), the final volume of his five-volume history of American writers, Van Wyck Brooks called *The Awakening* the "one novel of the nineties in the South that should have been remembered, one small perfect book that mattered more than the whole life-work of many a prolific writer."[12]

In the summer of 1956 Kenneth Eble published an important "recovery" piece in *Western Humanities Review*. He called *The Awakening* "a first-rate novel" and praised "its general excellence." It is also in this article that Eble made the well-known remark, "Quite frankly, the book is about sex." But unlike many other critics, Eble did not scold Chopin for choosing this theme. He ended his review with a plea: "*The Awakening* deserves to be restored and to be given its place among novels worthy of preservation."[13] George Arms later said of Eble's essay, "I think that it is fair to say that for most mid-century readers Kenneth Eble rediscovered the novel in his essay in 1956."[14] Eble helped prepare the important 1964 Capricorn paperback edition of *The Awakening*, introducing it with an essay much like his *Western Humanities Review* article.

The 1960s prompted articles by major figures of American letters, not only George Arms but also critics like Larzer Ziff and Lewis Leary. Ziff understood the novel perhaps better than had anyone before him, calling it "the most important piece of fiction about the sexual life of a woman written to date in America" (304). Lewis Leary demonstrated interest in the comprehensive reassessment of Chopin's career and canon in a 1968 essay on *At Fault* for *Southern Literary Journal*.[15]

Not surprisingly, this politically volatile decade also saw the emergence of a particular concern with women's roles and identities by scholars like Marie Fletcher and Joan Zlotnick. For example, Zlotnick picked up where Ziff had left off: in a 1968 essay she traced Chopin's motif of female defiance in *The Awakening* to short stories like "In Sabine" (1894), "Juanita" (1895), "A Pair of Silk Stockings" (1897), and "A Respectable Woman" (1894).[16] Like Lewis Leary, Zlotnick anticipated the modern reassessment of Chopin's other fiction. (The April 1993 Third Kate Chopin Conference at Northwestern State University of Louisiana in Natchitoches, Louisiana, for example, had as its theme "Kate Chopin's Other Fiction," and featured Barbara Ewell's insightful speech, "Making Places: Kate Chopin and the Art of the Short Story.")

The Awakening was also mentioned in popular magazines during the 1960s. On 23 March 1963, Edmund Wilson referred to Chopin and the misfortune of her neglect in an article for the *New Yorker*. Stanley Kauffman reviewed Larzer Ziff's book for the *New Republic* in 1966, making an extremely strong appeal for a Chopin revival. Inspired by Ziff to read Chopin's novel, he was overwhelmed by its importance and the history of its neglect. "It is an anachronistic, lonely, existentialist voice out of the mid-20th-century," he told the *New Republic*'s large readership. He concluded, "To discover a novel of such stature in the American past is both a happiness and an occasion for some shame. Not many readers would claim to know all of American literature, but some of us like to think that at least we know the best of it. *The Awakening* has been too much and too long neglected."[17]

The year 1969 was a watershed year for Chopin scholarship. Per Seyersted, a young Norwegian who studied in the United States under

Arnavon at Harvard in 1959 and was enthusiastically supported in his interest in Chopin by Edmund Wilson, published several works that attracted new scholars to Chopin's canon. Besides a two-volume edition of Chopin's work, *The Complete Works of Kate Chopin*, he also published *Kate Chopin: A Critical Biography*, which remains an excellent and standard work, concentrating on both recovering information about Chopin's life and interpreting the literature she produced. Seyersted examines matters of style, symbolism, and character, offering new and subtle glosses at every turn. He admires *The Awakening* for avoiding a final truth and message, emphasizes the existential dimensions of the novel and Edna's character, and praises the book for being "as modern now as it probably will be in a still patriarchal tomorrow" (163). Seyersted published the same year the first selected Chopin bibliography in Louis D. Rubin's *A Bibliographical Guide to the Study of Southern Literature*.

The 1970s witnessed the appearance of numerous reprints of *The Awakening*, often accompanied by insightful introductions. Lewis Leary, who had written about the influence of Whitman in Chopin, as well as the importance of *At Fault*, introduced the 1970 Holt edition. In the same year, Warner Berthoff introduced the novel for Garrett Press. In November 1972 the entire text of Chopin's novel was reprinted in *Redbook* (there is, incidentally, a copy of this work in the Bayou Folk Museum, Chopin's home between 1880–83 in Cloutierville, Louisiana), and in the same year Avon prepared its edition. The year 1975 saw the release of an edition edited by Per Seyersted and made available by the Feminist Press. In 1976 Signet published an edition introduced by Barbara Solomon, and Norton made available the first critical edition, edited by Margaret Culley.

Dissertations on Chopin began to flood the universities. Young scholars, many of whom would later make book-length contributions to Chopin criticism, were doing the academic research that would prepare the way for the varied and complex responses of the next decade: individuals like Robert Arner, Emily Toth, Peggy Skaggs, Thomas Bonner, Bernard Koloski, and myself. Bibliographies were being prepared by Richard Potter, Thomas Bonner, and Marlene Springer. And in 1979 Per Seyersted, assisted by Emily Toth, presented the Chopin community with *A Kate Chopin Miscellany*, an invaluable work that contains unpublished stories, poems, letters, an excellent annotated bibliography from 1890 to 1979, and two extant diaries (including the 1894 "Impressions," rescued from an old family trunk by Chopin's grandson Robert C. Hattersley).

A simultaneous phenomenon in the 1970s—one that contributed to the aggressive rediscovery of Chopin—was the emergence of feminist journals and books. *Women's Studies* and the *Mary Wollstonecraft Newsletter* were founded in 1972 and quickly featured Chopin scholarship. In 1975 the *Kate Chopin Newsletter* was begun, edited by Emily Toth. (The name of the journal would be altered to *Regionalism and the Female Imagination* in 1977.) *The Awakening* was discussed in volumes such as *Images of Women in Fiction: Feminist Perspectives* (1972), *The Female Imagination* (1975), *The Faces of Eve: Women in the Nineteenth-Century American Novel* (1976), and *The Authority of Experience: Essays in Feminist Criticism* (1977). Authors of these discussions were working to provide more sympathetic and understanding views of Edna.

A few critics of the 1970s would argue that a political reading of *The Awakening* misrepresented its author's intent. Lewis Leary in "Kate Chopin, Liberationist?" (1970) attempted to show that Chopin was not crusading for women's rights and referred to her moderate positions in essays and poems and in her own life.[18] In 1973 Cynthia Griffin Wolff insisted that the book was not most importantly about "the woman question."[19] Six years later, Nancy Walker closed out the decade by arguing that Chopin had no intention of producing a feminist document when she composed *The Awakening*.[20]

Books, and collections of Chopin criticism, appeared in rapid succession throughout the 1980s and into the 1990s. Peggy Skaggs (1985) and Barbara Ewell (1986) published book-length studies of Chopin. Harold Bloom edited a volume on Chopin in Chelsea House's Modern Critical Views Series in 1987. Bernard Koloski gave the scholarly community *Approaches to Teaching Chopin's "The Awakening"* in 1988; Wendy Martin's *New Essays on "The Awakening"* was released in the same year. In 1990 Northwestern State University Press released *Perspectives on Kate Chopin: Proceedings of the Kate Chopin International Conference*. Lynda Boren and Sara deSaussure Davis's

Critical Reception

Kate Chopin Reconsidered: Beyond the Bayou was issued by Louisiana State University Press in 1992. Also in 1992, Marilyn Hoder-Salmon's *Kate Chopin's "The Awakening": Screenplay as Interpretation* was released by the University Press of Florida. The year 1990 witnessed the publication of Emily Toth's biography, which features new stories about Chopin from family members and people in the various communities where she lived. Some of those relatives who knew Chopin, such as Julia "July" Breazeale Waters and Carmen Breazeale, died before the book's appearance, and we sense that Toth's biography may be the last one capable of capturing Chopin's life with the immediacy and intimacy possible only through such acquaintances. Toth's biography, informed by her extensive Chopin scholarship as well as by her feminist perspective, discloses significant details about the "banning" and about the mysterious figure of Albert Sampire, Chopin's rumored lover.

Essays and chapters about *The Awakening* or about Chopin have appeared in general collections with greater and greater frequency and prominence. Studies of Chopin have been included in volumes such as *Women and Language in Literature and Society* (1980), *Tomorrow Is Another Day: The Woman Writer in the South 1859–1936* (1981), *Portrait of the Artist as a Young Woman* (1983), *The Voyage in: Fictions of Female Development* (1983), *After the Vows Were Spoken: Marriage in American Literary Realism* (1984), *Feminist Dialogics: A Theory of Failed Community* (1988), *The Modern American Novella* (1989), *Women on the Color Line: Evolving Stereotypes and the Writings of George Washington Cable, Grace King, Kate Chopin* (1989), *Gender, Race, and Region in the Writings of Grace King, Ruth McEnery Stuart, and Kate Chopin* (1989), *The Green American Tradition: Essays and Poems for Sherman Paul* (1989), *Verging on the Abyss: The Social Fiction of Kate Chopin and Edith Wharton* (1990), and *Sister's Choice* (1991). In addition, new and revised bibliographies were published in the 1980s, including those prepared by Marlene Springer, Tonette Bond Inge, and Barbara Gannon.

What, then, are today's dominant critical theories about Edna Pontellier? To begin with, one school of critics echoes the assessment of Edna in the 1930s by Arthur Hobson Quinn and in the 1970s by

Cynthia Griffin Wolff and George Spangler: Edna regresses emotionally over the course of the story; Edna gives in to utter infantile selfishness. James H. Justus in "The Unawakening of Edna Pontellier" (1978) continues this interpretation.[21] Others, as we will see, remove Edna from the company of the great romantics, finding her little more than a love-sick fool, too susceptible to romantic love for her own good.

Some see her as impossibly trapped by the very system she opposes. Lawrence Thornton concludes that Chopin's text is very political, since Edna is deceived "by her private vision and by the society she discovers during the summer on Grand Isle."[22] In a modified version of this 1980 essay for Bernard Koloski's volume, Thornton compares Edna to Icarus and the labyrinth to the "plain of tradition" Chopin speaks of, the "labyrinth of social conventions, marriage, and motherhood that is closing around her like a vise."[23] Michael Gilmore, writing for *New Essays on "The Awakening"*, finds both Edna and Chopin hopelessly constrained by the worlds they occupy. For Gilmore, *The Awakening* "marks a turn toward the anti-naturalist, self-referential agenda of modernism as a liberating mode of behavior in life and art," yet it fails because both Chopin and Edna are "trapped in habits of thought they oppose, conceptual systems that prove so pertinacious that they saturate the very act of opposition."[24] Linda Huf believes Edna lives as a "new woman" in an "'old' society, with its conventions, prejudices, and superstitions." Huf calls her "too small a David to fell the Goliath of convention."[25]

Some feminist criticism has come at the problem of social and political constraint from a more specialized angle. In 1976 Emily Toth saw *The Awakening* as feminist criticism in the form of fiction, and Edna as "the embodiment of nineteenth-century feminist criticism."[26] She connected Chopin's feminist theory in her novel to that of Margaret Fuller, Charlotte Perkins Gilman, August Bebel, and John Stuart Mill, focusing on Edna as a case study of each social critic's concern with female confinement. Recently, other feminist critics have been more judgmental than Toth. Elaine Showalter, for example, points to Edna's addictions to "fantasy, money, and patriarchy." She describes Edna's "ineffectuality" in moving "from her own questioning to the larger social statement that is feminism" and attributes it in part to Edna's time, registering sympathy similar to Gilmore's and Thornton's. Showalter wishes, nonetheless, that Edna could recognize her connection with other women, could escape her fondness both for men and for solitude.[27] Others, such as Andrew Delbanco (1988) and Katherine Kearns (1991), have discussed Edna's unfortunate decision to pattern herself on a male definition of selfhood.[28]

Many recent critics have concentrated especially hard on the trap of motherhood. Peggy Skaggs believes that Edna discovers "that her role of mother also makes impossible her continuing development as a autonomous individual."[29] Patricia Hopkins Lattin demonstrates that childbirth and motherhood are positive experiences only in Chopin stories in which "a woman either will never have a child or has not yet had one." Works in which childbirth actually occurs—like *The Awakening*—offer "a pessimistic, negative view of childbirth and motherhood." In Chopin's fiction, Lattin concludes, motherhood "generally proves disastrous, causing insanity, death, and—of more significance to Chopin—a woman's loss of self."[30]

Other contemporary critics have emphasized Edna's role as a bold—and successful—heroine. Eble introduced this approach in the 1950s by comparing Edna's situation to that of Phaedra. "Phaedra's struggle with elemental passion in the *Hippolytus* is not usually regarded as being either morally offensive or insignificant. Mrs. Pontellier, too, has the power, the dignity, the self-possession of a tragic heroine" (268), he wrote. Sandra Gilbert argues that Edna is a Venus/Aphrodite figure, "a radiant symbol of the erotic liberation that turn-of-the-century women had begun to allow themselves to desire."[31]

Critics influenced by theories of language and patterns and modes of discourse have admired Edna's struggle to find her own voice. Scholars such as Paula Treichler, Dale Bauer, Patricia Yaeger, and also Michael Gilmore, sometimes using theorists like Michel Foucault for support, have taken on the difficult task of describing Edna's search for speech and language in a world dominated by normative patriarchal patterns. Reprinted essays by Treichler and Yaeger are among the five contemporary critical perspectives included by Nancy Walker in her 1993 Bedford Books of St. Martin's Press edition of *The Awakening*.

Several critics believe the book's most modern feature is its ambiguity, a major source of revisionist interest in Chopin's novel. In 1986 Barbara Ewell praised the novel's ability to yield few final answers. "Even now," she wrote, "withholding its own judgments, the novel quietly implicates us in its probing of such moral questions as the nature of sexuality, selfhood, and freedom, the meaning of adultery and suicide, and the relationship between biological destiny and personal choice."[32] In her contribution to *New Essays on "The Awakening"*, Cristina Giorcelli calls it a book that structurally and thematically "takes a many-sided perspective and allows a number of options to coexist and play off against one another."[33] And Marilynne Robinson, in her introduction to the 1988 Bantam edition of the novel, praises *The Awakening* for being "interrogatory rather than declarative . . . more inclined to inquiry than to statement," for its ability "to expound mystery rather than to dispel it."[34] New approaches to *The Awakening*, informed by history, economics, philosophy, psychology, and sociology, as well as by movements such as the New Historicism, feminism, and poststructuralism, appear with great frequency on editors' desks.

One group of critics has responded to *The Awakening* by comparing it to other novels. For example, Susan Rosowski (1979) has connected it to other novels of awakening: Gustave Flaubert's *Madame Bovary* (1857), Willa Cather's *My Mortal Enemy* (1926), Agnes Smedley's *Daughter of Earth* (1929), and George Eliot's *Middlemarch* (1871). In 1983 Priscilla Leder compared cultural conflict in *The Awakening* and in Herman Melville's *Typee* (1846).[35] Other critics have compared Chopin to George Sand, Sarah Orne Jewett, Edith Wharton, Leopoldo Alas (Clarin), Lafcadio Hearn, Margaret Drabble, and Margaret Atwood.

Publishers have aggressively continued to make original work by Chopin available. Numerous new collections of Chopin fiction, usually featuring *The Awakening*, were published in the 1980s by Modern Library, Bantam, Penguin, and Random House. In 1986 a paperback edition of *At Fault* was issued by Green Street Press, a gesture that stands in stark contrast to Chopin's publication of this text at her own expense in 1890. Previously unpublished manuscripts have also been made available. In 1988 Thomas Bonner published *The Kate Chopin*

Companion, with Chopin's Translations from French Fiction. In 1991 Emily Toth produced an edition of *A Vocation and a Voice* for Penguin, Chopin's third short story collection that Herbert S. Stone had declined to print. Emily Toth and Per Seyersted are currently working on a volume entitled *Kate Chopin's Private Papers*, to be published by Indiana University Press.

The critical attention given to *The Awakening* since its translation into French in 1953 by Cyrille Arnavon and its 1964 American reprint by Capricorn, promoted by Kenneth Eble, has been extensive. During the last half of the twentieth century, Chopin's novel has become one of the most popular and talked about books in American literature. Cathy Davidson, editor of *American Literature*, recently wrote in her foreword to *Kate Chopin Reconsidered: Beyond the Bayou*, "I have not done a quantitative analysis, but it certainly seems that we receive essays on Chopin with nearly the same frequency as those on Melville, James, and Faulkner. It is a rare month that goes by without a submission on Chopin and an unusual issue that does not contain an article, note, book review, or allusion to Chopin's work. In less than a generation, she has gone from obscurity to canonization."[36]

In 1980 the book's popularity was registered by the appearance of a *Cliffs Notes* volume written by Kay Carey. Radio adaptations and films of Chopin's fiction have been produced. Although no film project has been especially successful, both "The Story of an Hour" and *The Awakening* have each already inspired both a film and a remake. The second film of *The Awakening*, entitled *Grand Isle* and starring Kelly McGillis, was aired on TNT on 14 July 1992.

Enough time has passed since the book's extraordinary exclusion from the American canon to know that its popularity and tremendous appeal are no longer linked to the surprise of its discovery, or to the guilt of a neglectful critical community. *The Awakening* compels critics and general readers because it remains remarkably relevant, overwhelmingly vague and mysterious, beautiful in form and style—a book that matures as we mature and speaks greater and greater truth to us each time we open its pages. It is a book with nearly as many meanings as readers, and a book that, ironically, is even more controversial today than it was in 1899.

A READING

Esplanade Avenue, New Orleans, 1895. Chopin referred to the Avenue as Esplanade Street in her novel. Courtesy of *The Historic New Orleans Collection (acc. no. 1974.25.8.234)*

4

"A Green and Yellow Parrot . . ."

Imitative behavior was something Kate Chopin persistently fought. She smoked Cuban cigarettes, renounced the staunch Catholicism of her youth, and resigned from St. Louis's prestigious Wednesday Club after only two years of membership. In her essays of the 1890s she repeatedly insisted that writers be like Maupassant, a favorite author of hers who "had escaped from tradition and authority, who had entered into himself and looked out upon life through his own being and with his own eyes." Maupassant appealed to Chopin precisely because he did not appeal to the crowd, because, as she explained, "he has never seemed to me to belong to the multitude, but rather to the individual."[1] And in her fiction, of course, Chopin discovered her own impressionistic and uncannily modern style, choosing throughout the 1890s subjects and themes that would lead to rejections by conservative nineteenth-century editors, such as *Century*'s R. W. Gilder.

In the early chapters of *The Awakening* Chopin prepares us symbolically to understand that Edna Pontellier will try to find her own way, will try to abandon the unconscious imitation that has too often, and for too long, determined how she has lived. Edna Pontellier spends the last seasons of her life searching for knowledge of herself. She hopes, she says, "to realize her position in the universe as a human being, and to recognize her relations as an individual to the world within and about her" (14–15).

Although Edna does not find all the answers some critics have wished she might find, she begins to understand herself in a way that moves us and that predicts future examinations of women's roles in the history and literature of the twentieth century.

A green and yellow parrot appears in the first line of the book. Although Chopin refers to the bird as "he"—perhaps a deliberately ironic touch (Chopin knows from her first sentence that the spirits of men and women are really not so different)—scholars seldom interpret "his" situation as anything but female. Wendy Martin, for example, sees him as a symbol of domesticity, a wild bird "tamed for the amusement of the household."[2] As such a symbol, he becomes part of a symbol pattern that had been historically very common in women's literature.

For example, Anne Finch in "The Bird and the Arras" (1702?) relates the story of a bird that is fooled by the pictured scene on a tapestry: the bird, which Finch interestingly calls a "she," flies above the embroidered sky, thinking herself free, but sharply hits a "Cealing" that "strikes her to the ground."[3] The limitations of a domestic room defeat her after all.

Elizabeth Barrett Browning introduces the caged bird image as a symbol of domestic restriction in *Aurora Leigh* (1857), her long and rich poem about a woman searching for what is true. Aurora describes her conventional aunt as a caged bird:

> She had lived
> A sort of cage-bird life, born in a cage,
> Accounting that to leap from perch to perch
> Was act and joy enough for any bird.

Aurora, wanting more of life, sees herself as a wild creature that her English aunt tries to domesticate.

I, alas,
A wild bird scarcely fledged, was brought to her cage,
And she was there to meet me. Very kind.
Bring the clean water; give out the fresh seed.[4]

The metaphors Aurora uses for herself and her poetry are those of the falcon and the eagle. At the turn of the century Mary Elizabeth Coleridge used the falcon and the eagle in her poem "The White Women" (1900) to emphasize the strength of the legendary women of Malay: the very sight of these wild, tall, fair women causes the tiger, the falcon, and the eagle to "quail" (certainly a deliberate verb choice).[5]

Ellen Moers discusses the traditional use of bird imagery in the literature of women writers in her *Literary Women: The Great Writers* (1976) and mentions Chopin. She finds a striking absence of references in literature by women of what she calls "the nesting-bird for motherhood"; modern writers, she contends, know that "birds are frightening and monstrous as well as tiny and sweet." Monstrous or fearsome birds commonly enter "the grotesqueries of modern women's literature," according to Moers.

Moers notices the presence of the nesting-bird in Chopin's description of Adèle Ratignolle, and "the bitterness with which it is used to imply rejection of the maternal role."[6] We ourselves cannot help sensing this "bitterness" as we read through Chopin's description of Adèle: "It was easy to know them, fluttering about with extended, protecting wings when any harm, real or imaginary, threatened their precious brood. They were women who idolized their children, worshiped their husbands, and esteemed it a holy privilege to efface themselves as individuals and grow wings as ministering angels" (10). Women in the Creole community could have wings, but not for flight. Their wings were the holy wings of loving service to husband and children.

Chopin's selection of the parrot to hint at Edna's dilemma has significance beyond its representation of her caged condition, however.[7] First, unlike other caged birds Chopin might have selected, the parrot (probably a yellow-naped Amazon, though the makers of the film *Grand Isle* chose a macaw) imitates what it hears. Seyersted calls the parrot and the mockingbird "caged imitators, the one repeating its master's words, the other echoing the voice of other species" (159).[8] Symbolically, Chopin's parrot emphasizes the force and prevalence of imitation in society. Chopin's parrot speaks the language of the cosmopolitan New Orleans visitors who reside at Grand Isle in the summers. He speaks Spanish and French and English—but also, significantly, "a language which nobody understood" (3).

The parrot's language, then, is important symbolically not only because it represents Edna's tendency to imitate, but also because it hints at the need to discover and form new linguistic (and behavioral) patterns once mimicked speech has been discarded. Michael Gilmore describes the parrot as a "key symbol" in understanding Edna's desire for "authentic language." He observes that as Edna becomes less and less inhibited, less and less a mimic of those around her, she begins "to utter sentiments unintelligible to her companions," sentiments, for example, about a willingness to sacrifice her life for her children—but not to sacrifice herself (65–66). Patricia Yaeger, using Jacques Lacan and Michel Foucault, even suggests that the parrot "inhabits a multilingual culture and suggests the babble and lyricism bred by mixing world views."[9]

Like the parrot, most of us live and speak by imitation, as do most of the characters in *The Awakening*. So how will we know how to speak, or what to say, when we have only ourselves to listen to? And should we somehow miraculously be able to find the words and language that are ours, will anyone be able to understand us? Will we ourselves be able to translate our words into meaningful patterns, patterns of both speech and action?

For a parrot, and for a human being, freedom is not an easy matter. Like the domesticated parrot in the novel, Edna is vulnerable when she is free. She has been cared for too long by an owner and taught a language not her own. Also like a parrot, Edna has had her wings clipped so often that she will spend all of her remaining days trying to recover the strength and imagination it takes to soar.

Here, and in her other writing, the unattractive or comic depiction of the parrot reinforces Chopin's belief that imitation in our lives is detestable. The parrot represents Edna before she awakens: had she remained like the parrot, Chopin would undoubtedly have seen her as pathetic rather than sympathetic. In an 1894 diary entry from her volume of "Impressions," Chopin describes her personal aversion to parrots; this entry also anticipates her future selection of the parrot as a symbol for dullness and stupidity: "I have no leaning towards a parrot. I think them detestable birds with their blinking stupid eyes and heavy clumsy motions. I never could become attached to one. . . . It made me positively ill today when I had gone to pass a few hours with Blanche, to be forced to divide her society and attention with her own parrot and a neighbor's which she had borrowed. Fancy any sane human being doubling up an affliction in that way."[10]

Emily Toth suggests that there might have been a connection between this visit to Blanche (probably her cousin Blanche Bordley, according to Toth) and Chopin's decision to begin composing "Lilacs" (1896) two days later (1990, 238). In it, a "clumsy green parrot" serves a primarily comic function. We laugh at its name (Zozo), its stupid way of blinking at a young girl ("who was exerting herself to make him talk"), and its inability to compete with the chatter of Adrienne's servant and self-proclaimed counselor, old Sophie.[11]

In chapter 1 we are introduced to the Farival twins. The twin motif is another image of imitative behavior that, ironically, is also repeated throughout the book. Immediately after we are told that Léonce Pontellier hears the sound of "the chattering and whistling birds . . . still at it" (4), another noise from the main building is described. "Two young girls," Chopin writes, "the Farival twins, were playing a duet from 'Zampa' upon the piano." Here the juxtaposition between the parrot and the twins, a juxtaposition that will appear again, is first introduced. The twins play two duets over and over: "The Poet and the Peasant" by Franz von Suppé, and "Zampa," an opera by Louis Hérold that, as Culley notes in an annotation, significantly records a romantic death at sea. It is no coincidence that the performances of these pieces by the twins occur in the main building— the building where the summer guests eat and where, very appropriately, the parrot resides outside the door, like a sentinel. The twins soon become tiresome to the residents of the community, and to us.

In chapter 9, in the account of the party that precedes Edna's mystical and dangerous moonlight swim—a party at which the twins again repeat their two pieces—we hear more about them. Chopin describes them always as a pair, never differentiating between them. We learn they are 14, "always clad in the Virgin's colors, blue and white, having been dedicated to the Blessed Virgin at their baptism" (24). Chopin, of course, is in part poking fun at Catholicism and perhaps her own days at Sacred Heart Academy, something she does more than once in *The Awakening*.

Immediately after the twins' program is announced, Chopin ends a paragraph. The first line of her new paragraph registers what appears, very ironically, to be the parrot's own annoyance with the twins: "*Allez vous-en! Sapristi!*" (Go away! For God's sake!) the bird shrieks. "He was the only being present who possessed sufficient candor to admit that he was not listening to these gracious performances for the first time that summer" (24), Chopin humorously tells us.

Later that evening everyone dances except the Farival twins. Their inability to separate from each other has literally immobilized them, keeping them from pleasure, possibility, and promise. "Almost every one danced but the twins, who could not be induced to separate during the brief period when one or the other should be whirling around the room in the arms of a man. They might have danced together, but they did not think of it" (25). Their preference for imitation of each other rather than for individual growth makes them incapable of imagination. It is not surprising that their repertoire consists of only two pieces.

It is interesting that Chopin explores the twin motif in other works, as she does the image of the parrot. In "Boulôt and Boulotte," a children's story published in *Harper's Young People* in 1891 (a little too thick with dialect and rural stereotypes, perhaps, but nonetheless of some interest), Chopin adds an extremely important twist to the concept of twinship: one twin resembles her brother only in appearance—not in spirit. In a story that is very short and self-contained, Chopin shows her young readers the importance of stepping away from a twin—or, of course, from any person one has chosen, consciously or unconsciously, to imitate. Boulôt and Boulotte, two 12-

year-old "'Cadian" twins who reside in Natchitoches Parish, finally save enough money to buy shoes. On a Saturday afternoon they go shopping. A crowd of onlookers awaits their return. The group is amazed and confused because the twins are carrying their shoes. Boulôt flushes when he hears Seraphine, a 10-year-old neighbor, scream, "You bof crazy *donc*, Boulôt an' Boulotte. . . . You go buy shoes, an' come home barefeet like you was go!" Boulôt hangs his head shamefully, looking at the practical brogans that swing from his hand.

But Boulotte is more clever and resourceful than her brother—and quick-tongued. Her shoes, glossy and high-heeled with bright buttons, reflect her bolder and more demonstrative nature. Immediately "mistress of the situation," she replies, "You 'spec' Boulôt an' me we got money fur was'e—us? . . . You think we go buy shoes fur ruin it in de dus'? *Comment!*"[12] Though only a child, she is clearly related in nature to Chopin's daring adult heroines.

But unlike the twins in Chopin's 1891 story, in *The Awakening* the Farival twins are not meant to register the progression away from imitation. Rather, Edna is. We know early in the novel that Chopin is attempting to show that Edna has potential to be "different" from the crowd. Physically, she lacks the stereotypical, fashion-plate beauty of an Adèle Ratignolle, the quintessential Creole woman. Adèle is deliberately sketched by Chopin in excessively romantic and trite terms. "There are no words to describe her save the old ones that have served so often to picture the bygone heroine of romance and the fair lady of our dreams." Chopin must have been smiling as she continued to delineate Adèle's features: "the spun-gold hair that comb nor confining pin could restrain; the blue eyes that were like nothing but sapphires; two lips that pouted, that were so red one could only think of cherries or some other delicious crimson fruit in looking at them" (10).

Edna is different. "She was rather handsome than beautiful" (5), Chopin announces. *Handsome* is the word Chopin prefers to describe Edna, perhaps not only because it historically connotes, beyond physical attractiveness, a kind of dignity, but also because it has been comfortably applied to both men and women for centuries. Edna has yellowish brown hair and eyes and dark, thick, very horizontal eyebrows. Edna's actual physical features are briefly and quickly drawn, without extravagance and metaphoric lavishness, almost without interest. Some first-time readers might even have difficulty picturing Edna in their minds upon finishing the book.

What seems most important about Edna's face is that it hints at intelligence and depth. The eyebrows are distinctive, but primarily because they "[emphasize] the depth of her eyes" (5). Unlike Adèle's features, Edna's cannot be captured through worn-out and unsurprising similes like sapphires, spun-gold, and cherries. The language that describes her, like the woman herself, is necessarily more complex and abstract: her face displays, for example, "a certain frankness of expression," "a contradictory subtle play of features" (5). We are told in chapter 7 that "a casual and indiscriminating observer, in passing, might not cast a second glance upon the figure. But with more feeling and discernment he would have recognized the noble beauty of its modeling, and the graceful severity of poise and movement, which made Edna Pontellier different from the crowd" (16).

Chopin also sets Edna apart by letting us know in the early chapters that she is, quite literally, an outsider. She is not a Creole but has married into the Creole culture. Edna is from Kentucky, the daughter of a very gloomy Presbyterian minister. Her religion has cut her off from her own sensuousness; the lack of warmth and emotion in her sisters, her father, and even her friends has made Edna reserved and very private. She has not grown up with aristocratic Creole traditions and thus is both more curious about the culture and more critical of it than she would be had she been a Creole by birth.

After Edna speaks candidly with Adèle about her marriage to Léonce, about her susceptibility as a girl to romance, and about her uneven fondness for her children, it is no wonder that Adèle asks Robert for a favor: "Let Mrs. Pontellier alone" (20). She says, "She is not one of us; she is not like us. She might make the unfortunate blunder of taking you seriously" (21). She is not just voicing her concern for Edna here. Adèle is somewhat worried about the threat Edna poses to her own social order, and to the concept of Creole womanhood that Adèle has so completely adopted.

And we must wonder, when Adèle implores Edna to "think of the children" (109) in chapter 37, whether it is the children she really fears for or herself. Adèle's complete identity comes from her devotion to her children and husband. As Elizabeth Fox-Genovese points out, gender must be examined in Chopin's novel as a "social construction of sexuality"; gender roles in it "remain deeply hostage to considerations of class and race." To attack what would have been the South's views of women's roles—"daughter, wife, mother, nurturer, lady"[13]— was also to attack the superiority and the privileges of the white upper class. As long as women in the South continued to see their gender role as sacred (and Adèle is described as "a faultless Madonna" [12]), the deeply ingrained system of class and race would continue to survive.

Adèle is perfect in her role, but Chopin's irony reminds us always that it is, indeed, a role. In chapter 7 Edna succeeds in convincing Adèle not to bring her children along on a walk the two women take to the beach; nevertheless, "she could not induce her to relinquish a diminutive roll of needlework, which Adèle begged to be allowed to slip into the depths of her pocket" (15). We assume Adèle is working on the same sewing project of a few pages before: "a diminutive pair of night-drawers" (10). *Diminutive* is a word Chopin commonly, and perhaps somewhat unkindly, associates with the activity of Adèle: the little ones give her life focus and definition, but such absolute and rigid focus represents a diminution of possibility. And children's night-drawers, we might also note, impair development: they completely cover the child's body with cloth, except for two small eye holes. The role of motherhood, as we will see, haunts Edna throughout the novel and strongly influences her final act.

Edna, as we quickly discover, refuses to be a parrot, or a twin, or a representative mother-woman like her friend Adèle Ratignolle. Through the abundant irony Chopin brings to each of these images, we understand that Edna's refusal to imitate is correct and important. She will begin questioning the many assumptions her life has been built upon. She will examine more closely the domestic cage she has occupied. It has been a cage not unlike the one Mary Ryan uses as a prevailing historical metaphor in *Womanhood in America*: "invisible to the untrained eye, disguised by inviting draperies, perhaps even lined with little rewards and comforts" (15).

The image of the cage was present in "Emancipation," Chopin's first story, which was unpublished during her lifetime and in fact bears no date (though it was probably composed, according to Seyersted, in late 1869 or early 1870). The cage houses a large, sleek animal, and it opens one day by accident. The animal is clearly in greater danger outside the boundaries of his narrow world (though, we should notice, his danger is not as great as a parrot's would be), but Chopin applauds the risk of freedom. He rushes ahead, "heedless that he is wounding and tearing his sleek sides—seeing, smelling, touching of all things; even stopping to put his lips to the noxious pool, thinking it may be sweet." She concludes, "So does he live, seeking, finding, joying and suffering. The door which accident had opened is open still, but the cage remains forever empty!"[14]

The cage door in *The Awakening*, however, is a little different from the one in Chopin's very early allegory. It opens not by accident but through the persistence and courage of Edna Pontellier herself.

5

Keeping up with the Procession

In 1895 Henry B. Fuller published his novel *With the Procession*. Fuller was, like Chopin, "one of those 'lost' American writers who were destined to be rediscovered and lost again" (Brooks, 174). In his novel he explores the American dream of greater wealth, social ascension, and popularity. The comic Mrs. Granger Bates vocalizes the kind of ambition Fuller found so prevalent in Chicago in the 1890s. She explains her philosophy to Jane Marshall after showing Jane her "high art"—paintings acquired not out of passion but because "people of our position would naturally be expected to have a Corot." She proclaims, "Keep up with the procession is my motto, and head it if you can. I *do* head it, and I feel that I'm where I belong."[1] Larzer Ziff depicts the Chicago of the 1890s in much the same way. Looking closely at the World's Columbian Exposition held in Chicago in 1893, and thinking about the neglect and loneliness of writers like Whitman and Melville, who were still alive in 1890, Ziff concludes that there has been in America "a wholesale commercialization of life" (14), including the commercialization of its literature.

More than one author during the century's final decades was registering concern about American values, about artistic and social pretense, about schemes for speculation and quick wealth, and about the consequences of those schemes. William Dean Howells's *The Rise of Silas Lapham* (1885), set in Boston, is a well-known example of this genre. Howells offers the moral correctives of honesty and Christian kindness to the seductive lure of profits from Lapham's mineral paint formula.

Chopin used the phrase "the moving procession" in a short piece entitled "A Reflection," which she wrote in November 1899, six months after the release of *The Awakening*. She does not include a Mrs. Granger to define so exactly what she means by the phrase, but we certainly sense, through irony and contrast, that she wishes to depict the mindless energy of the great mass of people wanting "to keep abreast of the times." What she sees before her looks like a parade, but it is a macabre one. "Its fantastic colors are more brilliant and beautiful than the sun on the undulating waters. What matter if souls and bodies are falling beneath the feet of the ever-pressing multitude!" Those who march in it "do not need to apprehend the significance of things." But Chopin and Edna do.

With pretended humility, she places herself on the wayside, unable to keep up with the others: "Oh! I could weep at being left by the wayside; left with the grass and the clouds and a few dumb animals. True, I feel at home in the society of these symbols of life's immutability. In the procession I should feel the crushing feet, the clashing discords, the ruthless hands and stifling breath."[2] Emily Toth notes that Kate Chopin herself had traveled to the lake country in Wisconsin in October 1899, "escaping 'the moving procession' of St. Louis life, including preparations for Lélia's debut—part of the inevitable procession from birth to courtship to marriage to motherhood, all prescribed for a young lady in society" (1990, 362).

The procession Chopin observes in *The Awakening* marches through New Orleans, not St. Louis, Boston, or Chicago. But the rhythms are nonetheless familiar. Set in the early 1890s,[3] Chopin's novel in many ways is another satire of America's late nineteenth-century race for gold—a race that was literally acted out in the Klondike region of the Yukon between 1897 and 1899. Lincoln Steffens, Upton Sinclair, Ida Tarbell, Frank Norris, and other writers and journalists were exposing the serious consequences of America's crazed pursuit of wealth. But men like the fictional Léonce Pontellier would continue to grapple for profit. Léonce glances "restlessly" (3) over editorials and news when he reads his paper: the market reports are what really interest him. Rich Creoles like Léonce are so exhausted by the race for gain on Carondelet Street in New Orleans that they need their weekend vacations on Grand Isle to recover. Carondelet Street remains for them, nonetheless, the real arena of power and pleasure.

As Léonce knows so well, calculated social behavior is a necessary corollary to the Creole formula for wealth and success. For the New Orleans rich, conforming to others' expectations often directs and decides social conduct and etiquette: becoming part of the group depends on living by its code. It is not surprising that it is Léonce who reminds Edna of the importance of "keep[ing] up with the procession" (51): Léonce lives by mimicry—by buying valuable possessions that other Creoles will be impressed with, by investing money, by taking the right trips at the right time to make the right investments, and by lying when it is financially expedient to do so. When he discovers that Edna has gone out on her reception day, he gently scolds, "Why, my dear, I should think you'd understand by this time that people don't do such things; we've got to observe *les convenances* [social conventions] if we ever expect to get on and keep up with the procession. If you felt that you had to leave home this afternoon, you should have left some suitable explanation for your absence" (51). By "explanation," of course, Léonce means "excuse," tacitly encouraging his wife's deviousness. In his speech we also catch the ring of Judge Brack's words after Hedda's suicide in *Hedda Gabler* (1890): "But, good God! People don't do such things!"[4]

Léonce falls into a category articulated by Henry James in his notebook entry for 26 November 1892: "the male American immersed in the ferocity of business, with no time for any but the most sordid interests, purely commercial, professional, democratic and political." James believes that this situation has been responsible for the "growing divorce" between American men and women. And this divorce, he claims, "is rapidly becoming a gulf—an abyss of inequality, the like of which has never before been seen under the sun."[5] Not surprisingly, Larzer Ziff makes note of this remark at the beginning of his chapter on Jewett, Freeman, and Chopin, even entitling it "An Abyss of Inequality" (275).

In an essay that suggests Chopin's new critics have been no less severe than the old ones, Priscilla Allen explores the selfishness of Léonce in order to counter what Allen considers the misplaced critical focus on Edna's "selfishness." She does this by examining three "nagging" scenes, three "tantrums" Léonce exhibits: when he badgers Edna after he returns from Klein's Hotel; when he insists that she go indoors the night she learns to swim; and when he scolds her about not observing the social niceties of Tuesday receptions after the Pontelliers' return to New Orleans.[6] Linda Huf reviews these scenes in *A Portrait of the Artist as a Young Woman* (1985). Huf also asserts that Léonce is more selfish "than Edna ever dares to be" (63–67).[7]

Before Edna Pontellier can truly live authentically, she must step out of the parade that Léonce so casually expects her to join, step away from the procession that so swiftly beguiles and engulfs. Before she can discover who she is, she must rid herself of the social definition she has inherited.

We are told in chapter 7 that even as a child Edna had "apprehended instinctively the dual life—that outward existence which conforms, the inward life which questions" (15). For a while after she marries she talks herself into forgetting this duality: she plans to stop dreaming and very realistically become "the devoted wife of a man who worshiped her" (19). She will do what is expected of her. But during her stay on Grand Isle she begins not only to remember what she has always known but to rid herself of external appearances and habits she has thoughtlessly adopted and definitions of womanly happiness she has been taught by culture and society rather than learned through the painful process of self-exploration.

How the home appeared to others was crucial to men like Léonce Pontellier, men wanting to head the procession.[8] Léonce, sadly and ironically, cares only about how his home looks to people from the outside. He depends on Edna's help in this matter and on her "sense of submission or obedience to his compelling wishes" (32). His own personal success and prosperity depend on Edna's agreeable cooperation.

For instance, Edna, like other wealthy women in the nineteenth century, was expected to enjoy consumerism, to nurture the new industrial economy through her spending, and to help make her husband's financial success on Carondelet Street visible. But Edna likes to shop far less than Léonce does. At the beginning of chapter 18 Léonce tries to persuade Edna to meet him in town to buy new fixtures for their library. Edna responds, "I hardly think we need new fixtures, Léonce. Don't let us get anything new; you are too extravagant" (53). His answer is typical of other characters in processions throughout nineteenth-century fiction: "The way to become rich is to make money, my dear Edna, not to save it" (53).

A very particular etiquette accompanied the new consumerism. Etiquette books were a standard feature of a woman's library in the nineteenth century. During the six years of her marriage Edna has followed the rules of her class and of her sex that were prescribed in texts like Frances Hartley's *The Ladies' Book of Etiquette, and Manual of Politeness* (1875). Weekly receptions, for example, were automatic and routine. Hartley warns: "Let nothing, but the most imperative duty, call you out upon your reception day. Your callers are, in a measure, invited guests, and it will be an insulting mark of rudeness to be out when they call. Neither can you be excused, except in case of sickness" (50).[9]

Women arrived at Edna's house in the afternoon, placed their calling cards on a silver tray presented to them by Edna's mulatto servant boy, were offered liqueurs, coffee, and sweets by a maid, and were made to feel welcome by Edna in her drawing room. In the evening men could call with their wives. "This," Chopin announces, "had been the programme which Mrs. Pontellier had religiously followed since her marriage" (50).

As we have seen, when Edna stops this custom shortly after the Pontelliers return to New Orleans and their house on Esplanade Street, Léonce becomes genuinely annoyed. As he sorts through the calling cards, we understand the true nature of his irritation. The possibility that Edna has been unkind or unfriendly is not Léonce's concern. What worries him most is that such behavior has a price tag attached to it. It is financially inexpedient. "'Mrs. Belthrop.' I tell you what it is, Edna; you can't afford to snub Mrs. Belthrop. Why, Belthrop could buy and sell us ten times over. His business is worth a good, round sum to me. You'd better write her a note" (51–52).

Edna's behavior in this episode illustrates not only her boredom with the assigned role of drawing room hostess but also her break from an even more pervasive and destructive tradition in the procession of womanhood. As Edna tries to explain herself to her husband, the word *out* becomes central. Edna is trying to redefine the space historically permitted and assigned to American women since postcolonial days: instead of staying "in," Edna prefers going "out." The larger world, prohibited to women, is the world she wishes to explore. Instead of accepting the strict confinement of a small, domestic universe, Edna denies the reality of the space created for her and pushes the boundaries far beyond the property line of her home.

> "There were a good many [callers]," replied Edna, who was eating her soup with evident satisfaction. "I found their cards when I got home; I was out."
>
> "Out!" exclaimed her husband, with something like genuine consternation in his voice as he laid down the vinegar cruet and looked at her through his glasses. "Why, what could have taken you out on Tuesday? What did you have to do?"
>
> "Nothing. I simply felt like going out, and I went out."
>
> "Well, I hope you left some suitable excuse," said her husband, somewhat appeased, as he added a dash of cayenne pepper to the soup.

"No, I left no excuse. I told Joe to say I was out, that was all." (51)

Both participants in this conversation seem to sense the vital importance of the word *out*, for it occurs repeatedly in their remarks. Léonce exclaims the word in puzzlement and annoyance, as if it bears great and almost frightening significance. Why would any woman wish to leave the beautiful world of silver and damask that he has created within four walls? Edna says the word over and over, using it as a kind of subversive shorthand for a process she does not yet fully understand.

Mary Ryan speaks about the division of space sensed, less articulately but no less passionately, by both Edna and Léonce: "[Women are] restricted, in one degree or another, from the more public, active, wide-ranging pursuits whereby men win wealth and glory. Women's time-honored role, providing physical sustenance for a small group, carves out for her [*sic*] a limited space within society, more domestic than social, more sedentary than nomadic, more constrained than free, and more private than public" (6).

Throughout the novel we see Edna attempting to move toward spaces to which women are not normally granted access. She moves, of course, from the large double cottage on Esplanade Street to the four-room pigeon-house around the corner. Some critics have noted the mild irony that Edna buys another house in order to flee domesticity. Elaine Showalter points out the further irony of Edna arranging a dinner party as her accompanying gesture of liberation. Showalter writes, "Edna may look like a queen, but she is still a housewife. The political and aesthetic weapons she has in her *coup d'état* are only forks and knives, glasses and dresses" (52). But we must remember that Edna recognizes few options at this time, that she knows little else besides another version of her own life, and that self-growth is a very gradual process that often requires some imitation, some parrotry, before more radical and original choices can be made.

Also, the purchase of the house and the party itself, however conventional they may appear on the surface, are given enormous symbolic import by Chopin. The house, as we have already seen, has the distinct virtue in Edna's mind of being less opulent, thus symbolically marking her shift from social to spiritual ambition. And significantly, it is a one-person residence rather than a family home. Bert Bender even argues that the house is linked to "the triumphant female pigeons Darwin describes in *The Descent of Man*—creatures who, like Edna, 'occasionally feel a strong antipathy towards certain males [and preference *for* certain other males] without any assignable cause.'"[10] And the party, as we will later see, is hardly an ordinary birthday celebration; more like a Dionysian ritual, an orgy, it is played out in the realm of myth rather than in the arena of social manners.

Edna also tests the conventional boundaries of a woman's space through her frequent excursions to the race track. It is not only her attendance at the track that might draw notice, however, but her behavior there. Edna is often flamboyant, reckless, and excessive. People stare at her in a way they do not stare at her companion, Mrs. Highcamp, who "remained, as usual, unmoved, with her indifferent stare and uplifted eyebrows" (74). From the time the horses take the field, it is implied that Edna behaves more like a man than a woman. Chopin writes, "She did not perceive that she was talking like her father as the sleek geldings ambled in review before them" (74). Her intoxication with the sights and sounds of the track causes the crowd to glance her way and even listen to her, as if she were a male authority. "People turned their heads to look at her, and more than one lent an attentive ear to her utterances, hoping thereby to secure the elusive but ever-desired 'tip'" (74).

Edna breaks economic boundaries as well as spatial ones. She attempts to earn money to free herself from financial obligation to her husband. Charlotte Perkins Gilman articulated part of the unspoken motive behind Edna's desire to earn her own money: "In no other animal species is the female economically dependent on the male. In no other animal species is the sex-relation for sale" (95).

Edna earns her own money by betting and by selling her paintings. "I won a large sum this winter on the races, and I am beginning to sell my sketches" (79), she proudly tells Mademoiselle Reisz. Some critics argue, from a Marxian standpoint, that Edna's pride in selling her work, in turning her talent into a marketable commodity, is constricting and destructive to her development. Andrew Delbanco, for example, proposes that her pride in selling her sketches is "double-edged" (which is essentially how Showalter views her purchase of the pigeon-house): "What in one sense is a tremor of professionalism—a feminist victory—is also a lapse into equating the expression of self with goods and services whose value depends on social use" (99).

But again we might argue that Edna is only beginning to try, and to understand, alternatives to traditional gender roles. What Delbanco calls a "half-life" might also be labeled a "beginning." While Edna does profit from "selling" her talent, she does so while sensing all along what money of her own can buy: independence and freedom. Cristina Giorcelli sees Edna's imitation of male roles (drinking like a man, talking like her father) as an indication of her androgyny. "Chopin," Giorcelli writes, "seems here to imply that an up-to-date goddess and a fairytale or romance protagonist should be both feminine and masculine (not like Adèle, who, being only 'feminine,' is a 'by-gone heroine')" (122). Léonce acquires money to have power over others; Edna acquires money to have power over her own life. Without it, liberation is impossible. Virginia Woolf, of course, would tell this to the world in *A Room of One's Own* (1929) many years later. Alice Walker, in an essay about Zora Neale Hurston and the poverty of her last days, would offer another powerful statement about money and art, at times uncannily echoing Woolf's words: "Without money of one's own in a capitalist society, there is no such thing as independence. This is one of the clearest lessons of Zora's life, and why I consider the telling of her life 'a cautionary tale.' We must learn from it what we can." Walker continues, "Without money, one becomes dependent on other people, who are likely to be—even in their kindness—erratic in their support and despotic in their expectations of return."[11]

It may appear too convenient, too easy, that some of the money that allows Edna to purchase the pigeon-house comes from her mother's estate. Inheritance, however, often through widowhood, has historically been one of the only ways women have come to know economic independence. Thus, Edna's economic power derived from inheritance links her to the important traditions of women's history. But the issue of inheritance from the mother also connects her to legends and fairy tales about female strength. Like Cinderella and other motherless daughters in folk tales, Edna maintains an important supportive connection to the woman who bore her. We cannot help but think of the beneficence of Cinderella's dead mother (a story no doubt familiar to Chopin from her reading of *Grimms' Fairy Tales*), who showers her daughter with objects of silver and gold from the hazel tree that grows from her grave, planted there by Cinderella.

There are numerous other assumptions about wives and women that Edna abandons. A devotion to Léonce like Adèle's to her husband, for example, is not possible for Edna. And we are certainly not to think that Adèle's druggist husband is any more charming than Léonce, or easier to adore. Chopin describes the Ratignolles' dinner table behavior: "He talked a good deal on various topics, a little politics, some city news and neighborhood gossip. He spoke with an animation and earnestness that gave an exaggerated importance to every syllable he uttered. His wife was keenly interested in everything he said, laying down her fork the better to listen, chiming in, taking the words out of his mouth" (56). Edna finds such scenes "colorless," and we are meant to also. When Adèle later registers her opinion that the Pontelliers might be more domestically united if Léonce made fewer nightly visits to his club, Edna is surprised. "Oh! dear no!" says Edna. "What should I do if he stayed home? We wouldn't have anything to say to each other" (69).

Edna also refuses to practice the domestic arts as prescribed. Adèle, as we have seen, sews with persistence, investing love—and duty—in every stitch. Edna paints, preferring a brush to a needle. Like Anne Bradstreet, she might have said, "I am obnoxious to each carping tongue / Who says my hand a needle better fits."[12] And unlike Adèle's piano playing, as we will see, Edna's painting is inspired by something other than the intention of "brightening the home" (25).

Keeping up with the Procession

Edna has considerable success disposing of traditional concepts of social etiquette, social ambition, and domestic obligation. She is glad to step out of the procession that so strongly lures others in the book. A far harder task for Edna, however, will be to discover something that is more true, more fulfilling, and more worthy of human passion than the empty rules and rituals she has courageously abandoned.

The Krantz Hotel, Grand Isle. It is believed by many that Chopin used the Krantz Hotel as the model for Klein's in *The Awakening*.
Courtesy of the Historic New Orleans Collection (acc. no. 1981.238.16)

One of the buildings of the Krantz Hotel.
Courtesy of the Historic New Orleans Collection (acc. no. 1981.251.10)

6

Goddesses and Mythic Scenes

Edna was raised on Presbyterian guilt. Before Grand Isle, we are told, "the mantle of reserve . . . had always enveloped her" (15). Edna wears high collars and large, heavy hats, unlike her friend Adèle, who dresses in ruffles and veils of soft fabric. She is embarrassed, even shocked, by Adèle's frank description of one of her *accouchements* (births of her children) to old Monsieur Farival, and by the ease with which others on Grand Isle read and talk about starkly realistic books. But the excessive physicality of Grand Isle, as well as the Creole women who occupy it, proves irresistible to Edna. She has lost touch with her natural environment, owing to the confinement to church and home that her father and her husband have imposed on her, both directly and indirectly. Charlotte Perkins Gilman talked about this very phenomenon, suggesting that dependent relationships have always removed women from their physical environments. "When [man] stood between her and her physical environment," Gilman wrote, "she ceased proportionately to feel the influence of that environment and respond to it" (61).

The summer that begins the book also begins Edna's exploration of her sexuality. Through central scenes that are full of symbols and archetypes that connect Edna to powerful women of myth and legend, we come to understand how sex empowers her. Simultaneously, however, these scenes begin to identify why sex will ultimately not be enough to make Edna happy. She explores sex as a possibility, as a way to overcome both the severity of her childhood Presbyterianism and the empty rituals of her Creole married life, but discovers that sexual liberation is only the beginning of something much greater.

Edna is Diana/Artemis, Eve, Venus/Aphrodite, and Ariadne. She is surrounded by symbols and settings that recall the woods of Diana, the Garden of Eden, the groves and vineyards of Dionysus, the labyrinth of Theseus. Ancient symbols of oaks and fruit and wine pervade the novel. The most mythic scenes, perhaps, are found in chapters 10, 13, and 30, though no scene remains untouched by the emblems and significances these three contain.

The moon that illuminates chapter 10 is not the moon of the colonial forefathers. In his wedding sermon *A Wedding Ring, Fit for the Finger*, published in 1750, the Reverend William Secker writes, "It is between a man and his wife in the House as it is between the Sun and the Moon in the heavens, when the great light goes down, the lesser light gets up."[1] Speaking about widowhood, Secker uses the sun as a symbol for the husband, and the moon as a symbol for the wife. The moon is weak, obliterated by the intense light of the sun. By contrast, Chopin's moon is magical, mystical, and powerful; it lights Edna's way in chapter 10, becoming her beacon and her emblem. Cristina Giorcelli notes the significance of the repeated references to the number 28 in reinforcing this association: it represents the lunar cycle; it is Edna's age at the novel's start; and 28 August is specified as the date of her swim, the date the Gulf Spirit supposedly touches her (138).[2] In this scene she swims farther out than she ever has before, having grown "daring and reckless" (28). On this moonlit night, we learn, "she was like the little tottering, stumbling, clutching child, who of a sudden realizes it [sic] powers, and walks for the first time alone, boldly and with over-confidence" (28).

It is a moon that has many faces and properties, like the goddess Diana/Artemis that it recalls. It is Luna, the goddess of the moon;

Diana, powerful goddess of the hunt and chase; and Hecate, deity of magical rites. Even the mysterious Gulf Spirit that Robert suggests might have chosen Edna that evening to walk with the "semi-celestials" reminds us of a version of Diana's companion Hippolytus (or Virbius), who followed, served, and worshiped Diana, or of Cynthia's Endymion. Importantly, the Gulf Spirit never appears unless "the moon is shining—the moon must be shining" (30).

The moon offers Edna a vision of possibility only goddesses have known. As she swims for the first time, "she turned her face seaward to gather in an impression of space and solitude, which the vast expanse of water, meeting and melting with the moonlit sky, conveyed to her excited fancy". The power of the moon goddess seems to be transferred directly to Edna for one brief instant on this summer night. She appears "to be reaching out for the unlimited in which to lose herself" (29).

When Edna returns to her cottage after her swim, she brings new power with her. We notice that her manner with Robert—as well as with Léonce, in chapter 11—has changed. She issues orders and speaks more honestly than she ever has before. To Robert she says, "Don't swing the hammock. Will you get my white shawl which I left on the window-sill over at the house?" (31). And after Léonce insists that Edna come inside, she responds, "I mean to stay out here. I don't wish to go in, and I don't intend to. Don't speak to me like that again; I shall not answer you" (32). Once more we notice that "in" is not where Edna chooses to go; her domestic cell can no longer contain the person she is becoming. We also notice that as she addresses her husband at the chapter's start, "her eyes gleamed bright and intense" (31). It seems as if she has absorbed the brilliant light of the moon into her new vision of things. She has become the goddess of the chase: strong, commanding, daring, and sure.

But she is also acquiring the properties of Diana the fertility goddess. Fertility was a particular and important attribute of this goddess of nature. As moonlight continues to stream into the text, Edna feels strong sexual desire for the first time. Resting silently with Robert, her feelings are new and erotic. We are permitted to know something of what passes wordlessly between them. Chopin writes, "No multitude of words could have been more significant than those moments of silence, or more pregnant with the first-felt throbbings of desire" (31).

The moonlight that accompanies the last paragraphs of sexual revelation in chapter 10 is ambiguous but attracts our attention through its mysterious repetition. Twice in a matter of only a very few lines Chopin records Edna's concentration on Robert with these words: "She watched his figure pass in and out of the strips of moonlight" (31). As we witness Edna's attempt to romanticize her relationship with Robert throughout the book, we wonder if she perhaps is beginning the process even here. The image of Robert passing through "strips" of moonlight is a delicate, decorative product of a romantic imagination. It forces us to think about the relationship between sexual and romantic love. Placing this fragile image next to a strong phrase like "the first-felt throbbings of desire" symbolically anticipates the problems Edna will have determining the relationship between sex and romance.

The associative landscape that surrounds Edna is clearly more one of sexual fertility than of romance. Sir James Frazer notes that Diana is conceived of as the "yellow harvest moon," responsible for "fill[ing] the farmer's grange with goodly fruits."[3] We can easily imagine Diana, or Edna, walking the islands, gathering fruits and flowers in her arms. Throughout the island scenes Chopin associates Edna's emerging sexuality with the island's natural abundance and sensuousness. John May notes that the local color of southern Louisiana is perfect for Chopin's explorations; "sensuousness is a characteristic feature of the setting," he remarks.[4]

The environment seems to sharpen the senses. The highly fragrant camomile is everywhere. The "stretch of yellow camomile" (4) that the reader, in chapter 1, sees Edna walking through to join Léonce seems as endless as Wordsworth's field of daffodils. As she proceeds to the beach with Adèle, "acres of yellow camomile [reach] out on either hand" (15). On this same journey to the beach there are "vegetable gardens . . . with frequent small plantations of orange or lemon trees intervening" (15). Just before Edna's swim in the mystical moonlight, the wonderful, primitive odor of Grand Isle again assails her. "There were strange, rare odors abroad—a tangle of the sea smell and of weeds and damp, new-plowed earth, mingled with the heavy perfume of a field of white blossoms somewhere near" (28).

After Edna leaves Grand Isle, one flower especially—"jessamine" (jasmine)—comes to represent and to document her sensual development. Saying good-bye to her husband before he leaves for his day in New Orleans, Edna "absently picked a few sprays of jessamine that grew upon a trellis near by" (53). Erotically, Edna "inhaled the odor of the blossoms and thrust them into the bosom of her white morning gown" (53–54). In chapter 30 the odor of jasmine pervades the Esplanade Street house, where Edna holds her Dionysian party and celebrates the new liberation she believes is about to begin around the corner in the pigeon-house. "The heavy odor of jessamine," notes Chopin, "came through the open windows" (88). Later the same evening Edna's refusal to accept the sprig of jasmine Alcée Arobin offers her symbolizes her disenchantment with the evening's sexual overtones. "Will you have a spray of jessamine?" Arobin inquires, breaking off a few blossoms (91). Edna, deeply disturbed by Victor Lebrun's behavior and her own confusion, answers, "No; I don't want anything" (91).

It is highly significant that in New Orleans Edna seeks retreats—as does Robert—that are natural rather than those built by humans. The garden of Catiche, a *mulatresse* who sells bread and fresh dairy products, is reminiscent of Madame Antoine's property on the Chênière Caminada, where Edna still more fully awakens. But the "small, leafy corner, with a few green tables under the orange trees" (103) also recalls the sacred woodlands and groves of Diana.

It is almost uncanny that the oaks that protect the coastlines of Louisiana islands and shade the elegant homes on Esplanade Street are the very trees most vigorously and persistently associated with Diana and her groves.[5] Frazer writes, "While Diana was a goddess of the woodlands in general, she appears to have been intimately associated with oaks in particular, especially at her sacred grove of Nemi" (170). Writers of Louisiana have traditionally portrayed the island oaks in very female terms. For instance, in *Chita* (1889), another tale of Grand Isle, Lafcadio Hearn compares the oaks to "fleeing women with streaming garments and wind-blown hair." He watches them "bowing grievously and thrusting out arms desperately northward as to save themselves from falling." Hearn affirms the literal truth of his metaphor: "And they are being pursued indeed; —for the sea is devouring the land."[6]

Associating Edna so powerfully with Diana/Artemis allows Chopin a wonderful stroke of irony that becomes increasingly important as the book moves toward its end. Something we, and Edna, at times may have forgotten has been built into the mythic structure from the start: in addition to her other roles, Diana is the patroness of childbirth. The figure of Diana reminds us of the painful nineteenth-century reality that sexuality and reproduction are unavoidably linked. Chopin's very particular description of the oaks, for example, begins to hint at the complications of sexuality for most women of the nineteenth century. Chopin's oaks that "moan" as they bend toward the sea (32) represent not only the female but, more particularly, the maternal female. They are, like Hearn's oaks, victims. But interestingly, Chopin's symbolism suggests that they are victimized as much by maternity (the consequence of sexual force) as by the sea (the force itself).

The oaks in *The Awakening*, then, acquire very maternal characteristics. Children, again and again, play croquet under their protective shade. In chapter 1 some young people of Grand Isle, including the Pontellier boys, are playing croquet under the water oaks. After Léonce leaves for Klein's, Robert and Edna chatter "about the wind, the trees, the people who had gone to the *Chênière*; about the children playing croquet under the oaks" (6). The oak takes on the protective figure of a surrogate mother. Even in the early moments of their infatuation, Edna and Robert cannot avoid the children. As chapter 5 begins to close, Chopin carefully juxtaposes her description of the seductive sea and breeze with a description of the oaks and the children. "The sun was low in the west, and the breeze soft and languorous that came up from the south, charged with the seductive odor of the sea. Children, freshly befurbelowed, were gathering for their games under the oaks. Their voices were high and penetrating"(14). Their voices, in other words, are unavoidable. The children's voices will reach Edna and Robert no matter where they hide. The oaks must forever suffer and forever protect. They seem, in both Hearn and Chopin, like broken, tired women—particularly mothers, in Chopin—who rest only that they may moan and suffer once more. Anchored, they can only endure their fate.[7]

It appears, at first, that Diana/Artemis, virginal and chaste, can have little to say to us about maternity in the nineteenth century. Even though virginal herself, however, Diana was heavily associated with children: she made women fertile and helped them in childbirth, easing their labor (one of her distinctive features was having been born to Leto without pain). The trait of virginity (especially pronounced in the Greek Artemis) is extremely informative because it emphasizes how pervasive the idea of maternity was in nineteenth-century America. Even the century's virgins were expected (like Diana/Artemis) to commit their lives to loving service of others. The idea of motherhood as the sacred role for women had a powerful hold on both the married and the unmarried.

Motherhood is certainly the role that Edna most fears. But she also discovers it is the role she can do least to change. She goes to Adèle's side when her delivery is imminent. Even as she tells Robert, in "her seductive voice" (107), "I shall come back as soon as I can; I shall find you here" (107), she walks out of her house to witness, with "inward agony," a birth, a "scene [of] torture" ([of] Culley's; 109). The issue of motherhood, as we will see, is so distressing to Edna that she cannot resolve it.

Edna wears the many faces of Diana/Artemis. She has the power of the huntress at the chase when she swims boldly in the ocean or commands Robert or Léonce; the magic and mystery of the moon goddess when the Gulf Spirit seeks her out; the sexual vigor that caused Diana's followers to embrace and marry trees and pour wine on their trunks (Frazer, 9); and the maternal face she grows to dread so deeply.

The scene recorded in chapter 13 at Madame Antoine's cottage on the Chênière Caminada depicts Edna as both a new Eve and a female Christ. Revising stories from the Old and New Testaments, with Edna at their center, Chopin suggests that cutting itself off from nature and the physical has diminished traditional religion. She certainly suggests that this is true for Edna herself. Even within this powerfully positive sequence, however, Chopin introduces the possibility of passion having a dark side through the character of Madame Antoine's son Tonie (a young man we have met before in Chopin's canon).

It is important that the chapter begins in a church. Michael Gilmore has noted that the novel's title would have caused contemporary readers to think of religious revivals, or "great awakenings," but the book, in fact, is "the narrative of an antireligious awakening" (61). Edna is overcome with "a feeling of oppression and drowsiness" (36) during the service. Her head aches and her vision of the lights on the altar is blurred. She quickly rises and leaves, escaping the "stifling atmosphere" (36) for the fresh air outside. As in her parodic description of the Farival twins dressed in the Virgin's colors, certainly here Chopin is again depicting something of her disillusionment with formal Catholicism.

Edna first becomes aware of her own beauty in a setting quite the opposite of the one she has just fled. Madame Antoine's rural and primitive cottage, where Robert leads Edna, is at the very end of the village. Chickens wander outside the windows. The "sweet country odor of laurel" (37) permeates the air. When they arrive, Madame Antoine is boiling mullets over the coals in a very large fireplace. As in the grove at Catiche's, orange trees flourish. Edna awakens to her own physical beauty and health in the most physical of environments.

Preparing for a nap in the little side room of Madame Antoine's cottage, Edna notices her body in a new way. "She stretched her strong limbs that ached a little. She ran her fingers through her loosened hair for a while. She looked at her round arms as she held them straight up and rubbed them one after the other, observing closely, as if it were something she saw for the first time, the fine, firm quality and texture of her flesh" (37). Then, satisfied and pleased with what she finds, Edna "clasped her hands easily above her head, and it was thus she fell asleep" (37).

She awakens much later, her sleep having resembled not the 20-year sleep of Rip Van Winkle but, rather, the sleep of the princess in Charles Perrault's "The Sleeping Beauty in the Wood" (1697). Like the princess in the fairy tale, Edna has slept a 100-year sleep. Robert knows this. He says, amused, "You have slept precisely one hundred years. I was left here to guard your slumbers; and for one hundred years I have been out under the shed reading a book" (38).

But Robert does not seem to know, or want to remember, the rest of the fairy tale. The king's son comes to the palace and awakens Sleeping Beauty. In Chopin's version the princess awakens herself. Later in the novel, as we will see, Chopin continues to revise the story of Sleeping Beauty, further compromising the power of the prince.

When she awakens, she is literally and symbolically transfigured. As she washes her face and dabs powder on her nose and cheeks, Edna notices her reflection in a mirror. Ironically, although the mirror, "distorted" and small, somewhat misrepresents her physical appearance, it captures her new spirit with absolute clarity. Illumination marks every feature. "Her eyes were bright and wide awake and her face glowed" (38). We might be reminded of the Transfiguration of Christ, marked by an extreme and odd radiance of face and garments.

Very quickly, other religious rituals and scenes are reenacted and revised. Edna finds a brown loaf of bread and a bottle of wine awaiting her. Almost sacrilegiously, hungrily, she tears the bread "with her strong, white teeth," a powerful, feral image. We know that Edna has no intention of making this her Last Supper. Of the broiled fowl that has dried up during her extended nap, Edna says to Robert in an almost biblical cadence, "If it had turned to stone, still will I eat it" (38). She is resurrected to a greedier hunger for life than she has ever known before.

In Chopin's version of the story of the Garden of Eden (a place name that shares a curious sound resemblance to "Edna"), the fruit is named, giving it a physical importance very different from the more intellectual content of the unnamed fruit in the Old Testament. It is an orange, a fruit associated with warm and exotic climates. And Edna needs no tempter to make her reach for it. After finishing her communion, "she went softly out of doors, and plucking an orange from the low-hanging bough of a tree, threw it at Robert, who did not know she was awake and up". An Adam, Robert is forever changed by her boldness. "An illumination broke over his whole face when he saw her and joined her under the orange tree"(38), we are told. It is not just the symbolic property of the orange, of course, but the very physical presence of Edna herself that pushes Robert toward knowledge.

But we must return to Tonie before we leave this sequence, and Grand Isle, so that we might take with us all that Chopin intends. In 1893, six years before the publication of *The Awakening*, Chopin composed a story called "At Chênière Caminada."[8] In it we meet several characters who reappear in *The Awakening*: Madame Antoine, Tonie, Madame Lebrun, and Claire Duvigné (who, we briefly hear in *The Awakening*, is the woman Robert had loyally followed for two seasons but who had suddenly died between summers). The story's focus is the passion of Tonie for Claire Duvigné.

Chopin tells us in *The Awakening* that Tonie does not return with his mother after Vespers because "he was shy, and would not willingly face any woman except his mother" (39). But if we know something of his background from his earlier appearance in 1893, we suspect that this is not entirely true. Although Tonie does indeed appear to be shy, his passions are wild and extreme. In "At Chênière Caminada" the descriptions of Tonie's physique hint at the powerful forces at work inside him. Physically, he seems half-animal, half-man. He possesses the equine face characteristic of satyrs and sileni, a face "too long and bronzed." With "limbs too unmanageable" (309), Tonie walks like a plodding, stumbling beast. At one point Claire Duvigné notices that he appears "as strong as an ox" (314). He is a man of simple pleasures. Tonie fishes and sleeps and eats.

We must add to his list of pleasures his desire for attractive women. After Claire hires Tonie's small boat with its red lateen-sail (the same one we hear about in chapter 13 of *The Awakening*), Tonie watches her with "shifting glances." He vaguely recognizes that he wants to possess and consume her in as violent a way as the sea possessed and consumed his father, who was lost in a Barataria Bay squall. Indeed, notes Chopin, Claire knows nothing of "the full force and extent" (314) of Tonie's desire.

Although Tonie returns Claire to shore after hearing the Angelus bell, "he was stirred by a terrible, an overmastering regret, that he had not clasped [Claire] in his arms when they were out there alone, and sprung with her into the sea" (315).[9] This is certainly a side of Tonie not fully disclosed to us in *The Awakening*.

Tonie, through his curious and perversely dangerous wish, resembles Poseidon, the horse-god of the deep who produced monstrous progeny. Tonie, Chopin tells us, "resolved within himself that if ever again she were out there on the sea at his mercy, she would have to perish in his arms. He would go far, far out where the sound of no bell could reach him" (315). In the final section of "At Chênière Caminada," however, we learn that this will never occur. In New Orleans in January, Tonie hears that Claire has died of a cold "caught by standing in thin slippers, waiting for her carriage after the opera" (316). Tonie is at first destroyed by the news. "He wondered if the news was killing him" (317). He goes to a bar and drinks whiskey. But soon his mood changes, for he realizes that Claire's death has kept her from other men. Perversely, he becomes increasingly gladdened by her untimely death.

Like so many quiet details in Chopin's writing, how we are to assess our prior knowledge of Tonie is ambiguous. Does he illustrate the dangers of repression that Edna avoids through her sexual awakening? Or does the story of Tonie hint that passion is a complex emotion and might have a dangerous side of which Edna is not yet aware?[10]

In chapter 30, the dinner party scene, we are again symbolically shown that although sex has been a positive and liberating force in Edna's life, exclusive pursuit of it poses dangers. Sex is an important beginning, but not an end; it offers only partial fulfillment. In the last chapter of the book Victor Lebrun compares Edna to Venus. Hyperbolically, he tells his friend Mariequita that "Venus rising from the foam could have presented no more entrancing a spectacle than Mrs. Pontellier, blazing with beauty and diamonds at the head of the board" (111). Although Chopin does not introduce the name of Venus until the final chapter, throughout her pages she has quietly been introducing parts of the myth of Dionysus and Venus/Aphrodite, twisting it in important ways with threads of the legend of Ariadne, to register Edna's growing disillusionment with earthly, physical love.[11]

Several critics have noticed parallels between Edna and Aphrodite, including Per Seyersted and Bonnie St. Andrews, but no one has provided so elaborate a comparison as Sandra Gilbert in her essay "The Second Coming of Aphrodite" (1983). Gilbert reads the novel as a "half-secret (and perhaps only half-conscious) but distinctly feminist fantasy of the second coming of Aphrodite" (45). Edna, she contends, is a heroine "as free and golden as Aphrodite" (61). Metaphorically, "Edna has become Aphrodite, or at least an ephebe of that goddess" (54).

Gilbert sees the party scene as "the tale of a Last Supper" (56). Consistent with this reading, she views Edna's failure, as well as the gloom inherent in the scene, as the result of betrayals (56–57). Chopin's novel demonstrates, "from a female point of view, just what would 'really' happen to a mortal, turn-of-the-century woman who tried to claim for herself the erotic freedom and power owned by the classical queen of love" (45). Of course, one thing that would happen is that she would be betrayed.

Indeed, there are numerous hints that a second Last Supper, a much darker one than we witnessed on the Chênière Caminada, is being reenacted in chapter 30. The wine and the 11 diners invited to sit around her mahogany dinner table (Edna was to be the twelfth) clearly suggest Edna's potential as a Christ figure. Gilbert concludes that Edna is betrayed (that is, according to Gilbert, permitted "no viable role" as a "regenerated Aphrodite" [56]) by typical end-of-the-century viewpoints: the conventional timidity of Robert and the moral and maternal reminders of Adèle.

Gilbert openly admits in her wonderful essay that her reading of Edna as the goddess Aphrodite is "of course hyperbolic" (58). Indeed, it seems that by chapter 30, even before experiencing betrayal, Edna has given up her ambition to be the goddess of physical love. Although we are meant to recognize the parallels between her and Aphrodite, Edna (and possibly Chopin herself) is at times less bold and hopeful about sexual freedom and desire as a final definition of the self than is the goddess she seems so often to imitate.

Chapter 30 is an extremely complex episode. To some extent, as Elaine Showalter suggests, Chopin's dinner party is like other dinner parties in novels by women, a "virtual set [piece] of feminist aesthetics, suggesting that the hostess is a kind of artist in her own sphere." And, as Showalter further explains, Chopin's Edna is not unlike Mrs. Ramsay in *To the Lighthouse* (1927), who "exhausts herself in creating a sense of fellowship at her table" (52). Andrew Delbanco calls Edna's dinner "one of the great parties in American literature." He believes "it ranks with the Coreys' Touchetts' tea at Gardencourt, the revels on Gatsby's lawn" (103). Edna's party, Delbanco feels, proves that "Edna's is to be a revolution in incidentals only" (102). But, as we have already noticed, the dinner party in *The Awakening* has more than feminist and political implications: it is also a very distinct mythic episode.

Young Victor Lebrun is desired by the female guests at Edna's party, all of whom, appropriately, are older than he is. While Edna looks on, they vie for his attention. As the evening passes, Mrs. Highcamp, Miss Mayblunt, and Mrs. Merriman finally engage in the irresistible play of dressing Victor like a woodland god, weaving a garland of flowers for his head, draping silk across his shoulders, asking him to sing, pouring wine into his mouth, wiping his lips with their handkerchiefs, and crying out their delight in his beauty. What is difficult about this sequence is being able to determine its tone. Chopin never intrudes, never directly tells us whether she approves or disapproves of what occurs during the dinner to honor Edna's twenty-ninth birthday.

Certainly what we witness is revolutionary. Here are three intoxicated older women, two married and one an unmarried intellectual "no longer in her teens" (86), all looking greedily for an opportunity to receive attention from Victor Lebrun, a 19-year-old man. Is Chopin's purpose, in part, to test the double standard and prudishness of her own time and culture by deliberately reversing the conventional pattern of infatuation? Could she be asking why such attraction to younger people is not as "normal" for women as it is for men? Chopin also quietly seems to be protecting the females in this scene by making easy accusations of infidelity impossible. The one husband present, Mr. Merriman, is made to look foolish and quite undeserving of another person's long-term devotion and respect. He is "a jovial fellow, something of a shallow-pate, who laughed a good deal at other people's witticisms, and had thereby made himself extremely popular" (86). He tells a joke about "a man from Waco the other day at the St. Charles Hotel," but, we are told, "Mr. Merriman's stories were always lame and lacking point" (87).[12]

The exercise of dressing Victor, of transforming him "into a vision of Oriental beauty," brings the women pleasure. Miss Mayblunt, the bright woman some even suspect writes "under a *nom de guerre*" (86), "[loses] herself in a rhapsodic dream" (89). The other women find joy and laughter. There is something very ancient about their game, something deeply reminiscent of Dionysian festivities. Chopin's description of Victor reminds us more than a little of the wine god himself: "His cheeks were the color of crushed grapes, and his dusky eyes glowed with a languishing fire" (89).

Judgment of this very erotic scene comes not from Chopin but from two of the men at the party. Ironically, the first is the very promiscuous Alcée Arobin. When he sees women expressing desire, actively and aggressively, he feels disgust. Certainly Chopin is poking fun at his hypocrisy: he exclaims "*Sapristi!*" (For God's sake!)—a word we had first heard from the parrot. A little later, after Mrs. Highcamp entreats Victor to sing, Arobin scolds her: "Let him alone" (89).

We must, however, consider the response of Gouvernail much more seriously than that of Arobin. Although Gouvernail appears in *The Awakening* only briefly, he, like Tonie, has had larger roles in other Chopin fiction, in "A Respectable Woman" (1894) and "Athénaïse" (1895), for example.[13] And we have come to trust him. He has "penetrating eyes," "quick intelligence," and deep respect for women. In the story "Athénaïse" he believes that a woman is free to love whom she chooses.[14] He would have nodded agreement with Edna's alarming remark, "I give myself where I choose." He is like the intellectuals in the American quarter who are his associates—"*des esprits forts*, all of them . . . whose opinions would startle even the traditional 'sapeur,' for whom 'nothing is sacred'" (444). He tolerates married people but generally looks upon marriage with deep suspicion. Gouvernail professes to feel no guilt about being attracted to married women. "That [Athénaïse] was married," we learn, "made no particle of difference to Gouvernail. He could not conceive or dream of it making a difference" (450).

Nevertheless, because he knows the dangers of not sharing mutual affection and longing, he fights to control his passion. He deeply desires Athénaïse, but she does not want him. He refuses to yield to desire. "So long as she did not want him, he had no right to her,—no more than her husband had" (450).

In the two lines from Swinburne's "A Cameo" (1866) that Gouvernail "murmurs" under his breath as Edna's dinner party progresses, we must suspect the kind of sensitive insight into character, women, and action he has exhibited before. His selection of these lines—which mention, precisely, the dominant colors of Edna's banquet, red and gold—immediately alert us that his intelligence is at work. "'There was a graven image of Desire / Painted with red blood on a ground of gold'" (89), he utters. The lines perfectly re-create the color and mood of the night: the golden glimmer of Edna's gown, the yellow satin cover under strips of lacework on her table ("strips" that recall the "strips of moonlight" previously referred to), and the yellow silk shades of her candelabra. They remind us of the red and yellow roses that Mrs. Highcamp weaves into a garland to place atop Victor's handsome head.

But more than Gouvernail's knowledge of poetry and sensitivity to color is revealed by his recitation of lines from "A Cameo." Although he has not been actively engaged in the frivolity of the evening, Gouvernail has been watching the scene and assessing it. He is aware of the rampant desire in the room. "A Cameo"—as the lines Gouvernail quotes suggest and those he omits even more strongly imply—houses the thesis that desire can be destructive and ugly. An image is engraved in blood on the beautiful gold ground. By Desire sit "Pain" and "Pleasure," both of which seem unattractive. Pleasure sits by his companion "with gaunt hands that grasped their hire." The tableau also shows "The senses and the sorrows and the sins, / And the strange loves"[15] that follow like ugly beasts, wings and fins flapping. Gouvernail senses a parallel between the scene in the room and the tableau in the sonnet and quietly whispers it to us. Margaret Culley notes that the Swinburne lines forecast the failure of physical passion to relieve Edna's solitude. "Placed thus," she writes, "the allusion to the rather brutal Swinburne poem about the insatiety of fleshly desire and the final victory of time and death over passion, foretells the impossibility of such deliverance for Edna."[16] Nina Baym, speaking more generally of Edna's sexual awakening, writes, "We are given to understand that like her financial 'enthrallment' to her husband and her emotional 'enthrallment' to Robert, Edna's sexual 'enthrallment' to Alcée Arobin (or any other male) is finally another impediment to absolute freedom."[17] Certainly this reading is further supported by the disclosure in this same chapter of Alcée's address in the city (in other words, Passion's address): Perdido Street. Alcée, and the people who follow him, are in danger of being truly "lost."

Gouvernail senses this dark side of desire. Bernard Koloski proposes that Gouvernail knows something that holds broad implications for the entire novel: "Behind the sometimes wild activities of the guests is the brooding presence of death."[18] Death, who stands behind a locked "gaping grate" in "A Cameo"—not unlike the "locked gate" (91) of Edna's pigeon-house—is a significant presence throughout *The Awakening*. Gouvernail senses the inextricable link between pleasure and plain, desire and death, and he quietly identifies the danger and futility of what he sees before him.[19]

We could say this is yet another censorious man registering his disapproval of female sexual autonomy. But Gouvernail is a man with an important history and function in Chopin's canon, a man who loves free women, and who murmurs his wisdom, after all, "under his breath" (89). Soon after his words from Swinburne are quietly uttered, the behavior of Edna Pontellier herself seems to reinforce them. Indeed, this is not a cameo that she would choose to wear.

Edna, truly in so many ways the goddess Aphrodite, watches and rules from a distance. She is "the regal woman, the one who rules, who looks on, who stands alone" (88). This is her party, and it is supposedly a celebration of freedom, of birth. But when Victor, after being asked to sing, imitates lines Robert had sung to her as they crossed the bay from the Chênière Caminada, Edna violently objects to his demonstration—that is, to the culmination of an elaborate sexual scene. She places her glass on a table so forcefully that it breaks against a carafe. Wine spills all over Arobin's legs and onto Mrs. Highcamp's gown. Edna pushes back her chair when Victor refuses to stop and places her hand over his mouth. He continues to misread her and kisses her palm. The guests quickly "conceived the notion that it was time to say good night" (90), and they noisily depart.

In chapter 28, which consists of one brief impressionistic paragraph describing what appears to have been the consummation of Edna's affair with Arobin at the end of chapter 27, we learn of a most difficult and important discovery that Edna has made about her sexuality: it is not necessary to love a man to enjoy him sexually. Significantly, this discovery is made in none other than chapter 28— the number associated so strongly with the lunar cycle, the Gulf Spirit, and Diana. Chopin tries to help us understand what Edna feels at the moment of this realization, though her feelings are never simple or easy to sort out. We know there was "understanding" that involved "conflicting sensations." Among those sensations, we are told, "there was neither shame nor remorse." However, "there was a dull pang of regret because it was not the kiss of love which had inflamed her, because it was not love which had held this cup of life to her lips" (83). In chapter 30 the dull regret registered in chapter 28 seems to have become more intense, more alive, more unavoidable. Though only half-conscious of her motives, Edna still believes that spiritual love and earthly love can be joined, that Robert should be singing the lines to her, not Victor.

Ironically, of course, we have seen Edna herself "desire" Victor. During her unexpected visit with Victor in chapter 20 she begins to enjoy his candid stories; "she must have betrayed in her look some degree of interest or entertainment" (60). As he tells about a beauty peeping at him from behind her shutters, "the boy grew more daring, and Mrs. Pontellier might have found herself, in a little while, listening to a highly colored story but for the timely appearance of Madame Lebrun" (60). And after he walks her outside to depart, begging her to remember the confidential nature of the secrets he has shared, she flirts in spite of herself. "She laughed and bantered him a little, remembering too late that she should have been dignified and reserved" (61). Though Victor disgusts her the evening of her party, his kiss on her palm "was like a pleasing sting to her hand" (90). Edna could have chosen Victor for herself the night of her party. The real Aphrodite did. In a brief affair, she bore the god Dionysus a son—Priapus, a god of undaunted fertility. But Edna is not Aphrodite.

Associations between Edna and Ariadne are also invited by the book, most immediately through the image of sewing and thread, as well as the visual picture Edna forms of a woman dancing between tall, labyrinthian hedges. The multiple versions of Ariadne's story (typical of so many stories in myth) allow us a more comprehensive view of Edna herself, and complement Chopin's ambiguous style. Ariadne, like Aphrodite—and Edna—is involved with Dionysus. In one version of her story, Dionysus (Passion) rewards Ariadne. After supposedly causing Theseus to forget her, he falls in love with Ariadne himself, marries her, and later sets a beautiful, golden marriage crown among the stars. She bears Dionysus many children. But in another version of the tale Dionysus destroys Ariadne for profaning his shrine by making love there with Theseus. In yet a third version Ariadne seems to choose her own death, asking Theseus to put her ashore at her request—apparently knowing she will die. Edna's celebration (complete with her own crown of diamonds), her victimization, and her suicide in the waters of the Gulf can all coexist within the wide boundaries of Ariadne's story—within the wide boundaries of myth itself.

In these three key mythic scenes Chopin shows us that Edna gains much through her sexual rebirth, but not everything. For example, suggestions of Diana, who functions both as a patron of childbirth and the goddess of fertility, hint that Edna will eventually have to admit that female biology can liberate, but that its reproductive aspect can enslave. Early on, she does not see—or does not admit—the connection between sex and motherhood. These scenes also help us understand her disillusionment with affairs, with relationships that lack spiritual content. They anticipate the conclusion Edna will reach the night before her final walk into the Gulf: "She had said over and over to herself: 'To-day it is Arobin; to-morrow it will be some one else'" (113).

Through the characters of Tonie and Gouvernail, as well as her revisions of familiar myths and stories, Chopin symbolically informs us that Edna's search for fulfillment does not end with her sexual awakening. Edna will look next to the romantic arms of Robert.

7

"Couldst Thou But Know":
Edna's Pursuit of the Beloved

At the end of chapter 30, as we have seen, Edna's desire for romantic love causes her to respond angrily to its perversion by her dinner guests, the Dionysian Victor Lebrun as well as the New Orleans maenads who follow and pursue him. Although there are clues throughout the novel that Edna will never be able to believe in sentimental love, it is clear, until the last few episodes of the book, that she wants to. "The beloved one," a phrase impossible for Edna to utter without a sigh, is the product of her dreams and imagination, as well as the creation of her times.

At her dinner party, "there came over her the acute longing which always summoned into her spiritual vision the presence of the beloved one" (88). Returning home after witnessing the brutal scene of Adèle's childbirth, expecting to find Robert, Edna "could picture at that moment no greater bliss on earth than possession of the beloved one" (110).

The sensitive but conventional Robert Lebrun becomes for Edna the embodiment of ideal and romantic love, her "beloved one." Eventually, however, she relinquishes her belief in romance, as she does many of the other myths of her age and her culture, moving still closer to authenticity and truth. Chopin carefully defines the sentimental romance characteristic of Edna and her century, showing its pervasiveness, its form, its power—both Edna and we as readers are embarrassingly susceptible—and its insidious, sometimes comic, always destructive effects.

In the novel's final pages, the wise Dr. Mandelet tells Edna, "The trouble is . . . that youth is given up to illusions. It seems to be a provision of Nature; a decoy to secure mothers for the race" (109–10). Mary Ryan proposes that the job of "the American cultural industry between 1830 and 1860 was to recruit the emotional energies of masses of women for a civilizing mission" (147). The task, in other words, was to create one of the illusions Dr. Mandelet knows is responsible for securing unions—and children—for young men and women. Between the lines of novels by women like Catharine Sedgwick and E. D. E. N. Southworth, Ryan observes, was the message that "love waxed ecstatic during the quest for a mate, not in the course of married life" (151), that romantic love "could disguise the inequitable relationship a bride was about to accept" (154).

Yet popular romances by women writers of the nineteenth century frequently became best-sellers. Successful romances written by 12 women writers Mary Kelley dubs the "literary domestics" appeared decade after decade. Kelley writes, "Beginning with Catharine Maria Sedgwick's first novel in 1822, they issued the largest number of their best-selling works in the 1850s, 1860s, and 1870s, and some of their books continued to sell widely into the early decades of the twentieth century" (viii). Mrs. E. D. E. N. Southworth wrote so prolifically that it would take 42 volumes to house her collected novels, romances with titles like *How He Won Her* (1869), *Little Nea's Engagement* (1889), *An Unrequited Love* (1890), *For Woman's Love* (1890), and *Sweet Love's Atonement* (1904).

Chopin, in her depiction of the "romance" between Edna and Robert, seems, again, on a revolutionary fringe. She supplies her readers with the romantic dreams they would expect from conventional popular pulp romance. But she also eventually forces both Edna and her readers to give up these dreams. In a review of Hamlin Garland's

Crumbling Idols (1894), Chopin warned Garland, and us, to test all literature, new and old, by only one standard: is it a "true" depiction of human impulse?[1] In 1899 Chopin could not permit Edna and Robert to come together and still be "true" to what Chopin knew and felt.

Edna has absorbed and adopted many of the traits of romantic nineteenth-century heroines and of the century's concept of romantic love. For example, she exhibits numerous romantic symptoms registered by other characters who fall in love in nineteenth-century novels. We can learn much about Edna's initial susceptibility to romance and the culture that fostered it by comparing her behavior to that of characters in Louisa May Alcott's *Little Women* (1860)—a sort of literary handbook for the instruction of the century's children. Jo March, deeply annoyed by her sister Meg's attraction to John Brooke, describes general romantic behavior as she registers her particular observations about her sister. "She feels it in the air—love, I mean—and she's going very fast," Jo says. "She's got most of the symptoms—is twittery and cross, doesn't eat, lies awake, and mopes in corners. I caught her singing that song he gave her, and once she said 'John,' as you do, and then turned red as a poppy. Whatever shall we do?"[2]

Edna exhibits many of Meg's romantic mannerisms. We learn of her early infatuations. Edna had been "passionately enamoured" (18) of a sorrowful cavalry officer and was unable to remove her eyes from his face; her affections had been "deeply engaged" (19) another time by a young man about to marry a woman on a neighboring Mississippi plantation; yet a third time she had fallen in love with a tragedian and kissed the cold glass of his framed picture.

Such symptoms return when Edna meets Robert. Like Meg March, she flushes uncontrollably. When she confesses her love for Robert to Mademoiselle Reisz in chapter 26, she blushes as severely as Alcott's little woman Meg. "Are you in love with Robert?" Mademoiselle Reisz bluntly asks. "Yes," Edna replies. Then we are told, "It was the first time she had admitted it, and a glow overspread her face, blotching it with red spots" (81). We might wonder if Chopin did not very deliberately select the word *blotching* here. This unpleasant word hints that there might be ugly, disfiguring consequences to romantic love.

Edna, also like Meg March, repeatedly clings to the melody and lyrics of a song Robert has given her, the song "Couldst Thou But Know." In chapter 14, after her return from the Chênière with Robert, waiting for her husband to come home from Klein's, "she sang low a little song that Robert had sung as they crossed the bay" (41). As we have seen, this is the song Victor mimics at the premature close of her dinner party in chapter 30. When Victor sings the first line—the line that ends each refrain, "Ah! *si tu savais!*" (couldst thou but know)—Edna cries out, "Stop! don't sing that. I don't want you to sing it" (90). Everything about the song is romantically sacred to Edna: "The voice, the notes, the whole refrain haunted her memory" (41). The song that so immediately attaches her to Robert, "their" song, was one of many sentimental songs written and sung by the popular composer-baritone Michael William Balfe (1808–70), further verifying our suspicion that Edna is sometimes influenced by popular culture.

Also, as Elaine Showalter notes, Chopin's allusions to the music of Frédéric Chopin help establish the romantic relationship between Edna and Robert. She writes, "These references to 'Chopin' in the text are on one level allusions to an intimate, romantic, and poignant musical *oeuvre* that reinforces the novel's sensual atmosphere" (47).[3] The music of Chopin has romantic intimacy and a power that seems capable of sustaining this mood.

Edna's attraction to tales and stories of the Baratarian pirates is a central device Chopin uses to further extend her exploration of Edna's romantic nature. The Gulf Coast culture is a perfect complement to it: it is full of legends, pirate stories, and tales of imaginary ships and gold. Edna's interest in stories of Jean Lafitte and his cohorts represents, in part, an attraction to legend, to what is false rather than true, to what is thrilling and pleasurable rather than spiritually agonizing.

Several times in the novel, for example, the subject of buried treasure is introduced. Historians of the Gulf Coast have frequently recited the romance that grew up around Lafitte and his treasure, finding it amusing and extreme. The popular Lafitte biographer Lyle Saxon records bizarre episodes of treasure hunting, including the dynamiting of trees on Pecan Island, 20-year searches that ended in drowning, and the abusive use of hypnotized children and servants to make discoveries. According to Saxon, Lafitte was too poor at the end of his career to bury any amount of money. The last sentence of Saxon's 1930 biography reads, "It is possible, of course, that in those earlier, gaudier and more prosperous times he buried chests filled with golden doubloons and Pieces of Eight; but if so, it is more than likely that he dug them up again."[4] The romance of pirates and pirate treasure is only real, in other words, until one begins to search for it. Helen Taylor also points to the irony (irony that she feels contemporary readers would have sensed) that "Chopin sets much of her novel on an island that she knew had been virtually destroyed by the 1893 hurricane" (177). Dreams, like the place where dreams occur, the place where Lafitte once divided up his spoils, would inevitably be lost.

Before Edna and Robert arrive at the Chênière, they talk about visiting Grande Terre and Bayou Brulow, and then share a fantasy of buried treasure that causes both to grow reckless in their conversation, and Robert even to flush. Edna, appropriately, prefers the erotic and romantic environment of Grand Terre to the more painfully symbolic village of Bayou Brulow. She thinks about being alone with Robert on Grand Terre, "in the sun, listening to the ocean's roar and watching the slimy lizards writhe in and out among the ruins of the old fort" (35)—ironically, the very place Jean Lafitte selected to defend himself from Captain Andrew Hunter Holmes and customs officials, and the very fort whose walls Lafitte himself strengthened.[5]

Bayou Brulow, we learn, is a place where people fish. When Edna discovers this, she announces, "No; we'll go back to Grande Terre. Let the fish alone" (35). What could this response mean? It is difficult to read this without thinking of yet another legend, one far more painful—the Arthurian legend of the Fisher King. In some versions of the story the Fisher King has a wound in his side that can only be cured by Parsifal's search for truth, by asking what is wrong. In the legends of the Holy Grail, wisdom is achieved only through suffering, through bitter and agonizing psychological exploration and struggle. It is more than a little symbolic that at one point very late in the novel Chopin describes Edna's need to resolve her ambivalent feeling toward her children as something that "had driven into her soul like a death wound" (110). The fish, of course, also might suggest to some readers the suffering of Christ, or the painful price of discipleship to truth.

Instead, Robert and Edna talk of treasure, like children afraid to face the reality of the day. Robert discloses the plan for preparing his pirogue and sailing in the moonlight to haunted coves. "Maybe your Gulf spirit will whisper to you in which of these islands the treasures are hidden—direct you to the very spot, perhaps" (35). Edna enjoys the game they play and answers excitedly, "And in a day we should be rich!" She continues, "I'd give it all to you, the pirate gold and every bit of treasure we could dig up. I think you would know how to spend it. Pirate gold isn't a thing to be hoarded or utilized. It is something to squander and throw to the four winds, for the fun of seeing the golden specks fly" (35–36). Later, Edna's imagination is further excited by the pirate stories of Madame Antoine. Sitting on the ground at the old woman's feet, "Edna could hear the whispering voices of dead men and the click of muffled gold" (39).

At the party for her father that Dr. Mandelet attends, Edna continues her dreams and fantasies. She tells the story "of a woman who paddled away with her lover one night in a pirogue and never came back. They were lost amid the Baratarian Islands, and no one ever heard of them or found trace of them from that day to this" (70). She tells her tale, born of dreams, with such intensity, enthusiasm, and romantic passion that her listeners "could see the faces of the lovers, pale, close together, rapt in oblivious forgetfulness, drifting into the unknown" (70).

Many times Edna dreams about Robert, very much in the way she dreams about pirates and gold. It is appropriate that Chopin often describes her dreams about Robert, for dreams are the place, the only place, where romance can exist. We are told that "a hundred times" (97) Edna had imagined her reunion with Robert, his searching her out immediately upon his return to New Orleans, and his ready confession of love. Even after the actual reunion, which is far less romantic, she continues to imagine Robert desiring her as he drifts through an ordinary workday. After picturing Robert going to his business, bending over his desk, and talking to his colleagues, she proceeds to imagine him walking to lunch while "watching for her on the street"

(102). Even after witnessing Adèle's labor, she tries to dispel the image of maternal suffering from her mind and heart, promising herself to think of such things another time—"but not tonight. To-morrow would be time to think of everything" (110). Instead, she pictures a moment of bliss with Robert.

In the most ecstatic moment of her dream life, Edna casts herself in the role of the prince in "Sleeping Beauty"—a story we first saw hinted at in the description of her nap of 100 years on the Chênière—as well as in the mythic role of Cynthia, the moon goddess in the myth of Endymion. Edna believes for a moment that she has the power to break spells, to grant favor, perhaps to bestow eternal life. Certainly Chopin's contemporaries would have recognized Cynthia and Endymion in this scene: in addition to John Lyly's *Endimion* (1591), nineteenth-century readers might have known John Keats's *Endymion* (1818), or Benjamin Disraeli's novel by the same name (1880).

Nonetheless, even though Edna is more powerful than she was earlier in the novel, she still embraces the romantic structure and possibilities of the story—for romantic union remains the goal of her gesture. "It was so late; he would be asleep perhaps. She would awaken him with a kiss. She hoped he would be asleep that she might arouse him with her caresses" (110).[6] Edna has momentarily forgotten the lesson she learned at Madame Antoine's: an awakening can not be brought about by another, but only by oneself.

Even Edna's conversations with Robert are often more than vaguely derivative of the style and language of romantic literature and sentimental poetry. After talking with him strongly and candidly in chapter 36, pronouncing, "I give myself where I choose" (107), and correcting his notions about fidelity and marriage, she lapses into unauthentic language and posturing when she takes her leave, language that reminds us of the parrot talk referred to in chapter 1. She says good-bye to her "sweet Robert" like this: "I love you . . . only you; no one but you. It was you who awoke me last summer out of a life-long, stupid dream. Oh! you have made me so unhappy with your indifference. Oh! I have suffered, suffered! Now you are here we shall love each other, my Robert. We shall be everything to each other. Nothing else in the world is of any consequence" (107). Edna's words read like Balfe lyrics. The sharp contrast between Edna's earlier speeches to Robert and her rhetoric here assures us of Chopin's ironic attitude toward romance, if we ever had any doubt.

After her reunion with Robert in Mademoiselle Reisz's apartment, it is clear that Edna is beginning to know the truth about the romantic union she so hopelessly pursues. Her dreams of a romantic meeting are severely compromised by "the reality . . . that they sat ten feet apart, she at the window, crushing geranium leaves in her hand and smelling them, he twirling around on the piano stool" (97). It is not at all what Edna had imagined it would be: dead geranium leaves and a nervous tension in her lover that threatens to twist him off the very stool he occupies.

Later that day, after Robert's visit to Edna's pigeon-house, she tries to recapture the romance of Robert. "She stayed alone in a kind of reverie—a sort of stupor. Step by step she lived over every instant of the time she had been with Robert after he had entered Mademoiselle Reisz's door. She recalled his words, his looks" (101). But the dream can no longer be so easily re-created; it can be recalled only in "a sort of stupor." And the conclusion of the dream is cynicism, not hope and joy and exultation. "She had been with him, had heard his voice and touched his hand. But some way he had seemed nearer to her off there in Mexico" (102). What Edna is coming to know, of course, is that romance can *only* be dreamed, not lived.

In a second conversation between Edna and Robert (the one she concludes by announcing she will give herself where she chooses) we come to understand even more about Edna's final decision to give up romance. In it she radically modifies the nineteenth-century formula—in ways that Robert can neither accept nor imagine. Robert dreams of writing the same ending for his life that sentimental novels of love were prescribing. Like the characters in novels of the period, Robert sees marriage as the natural consequence of his strong affection for Edna. He says, "Something put into my head that you cared for me; and I lost my senses. I forgot everything but a wild dream of your some way becoming my wife" (106). She exclaims, "Your wife!" Edna is pursuing romance for its own sake, not because it will lead to marriage. She has, then, outgrown some of the components of the romantic formula provided by the popular literature and social conventions of the nineteenth century. Edna refuses to end her own story in the way of romantic novels—we are never to believe that even if Robert had bravely remained Edna would have chosen to marry him. Yet, because she has no pattern, no map in hand, no preconceived idea about the end results, she must discover on her own where romance truly leads.

At the end of the novel Edna makes one of her boldest statements to Dr. Mandelet: "The years that are gone seem like dreams—if one might go on sleeping and dreaming—but to wake up and find—oh! well! perhaps it is better to wake up after all, even to suffer, rather than to remain a dupe to illusions all one's life" (110). One of the illusions Edna gives up, an illusion Chopin herself relinquishes in her decision not to write in the tradition of the literary domestics, is the belief in romantic, sentimental love. It is painful for both Chopin and Edna to disinherit this belief. Robert's conventional departure ("I love you. Good-by—because I love you" [111]) is not what assures Edna of love's impossibility. She has known long before reading Robert's words that romantic love was, at best, a fleeting dream.

Edna wants very much to separate sex from love, to assure herself that her feelings for Robert have been of a decidedly different variety from those she has for Alcée Arobin. She must come to admit, however, that her attraction to Robert will be no more lasting or permanent than her attraction to Alcée—because romantic love, after all, is no different from sex in the world of *The Awakening*. Barbara Ewell notes, "Edna's confusion of romance and passion—and the comprehension that the experience of passion brings—is familiar in Chopin's fiction" (149). And Chopin is no E. D. E. N. Southworth. It seems a telling coincidence that the 80-year-old Southworth died in 1899, the year *The Awakening* was published. The year of Southworth's death, Chopin destroyed the tradition of the sentimental novel.

We often are drawn into the romance of Edna and Robert, perhaps wanting so much to believe it ourselves. But Chopin, through symbol and irony, warns us to be cautious. The pair of lovers floating through Chopin's pages, "shoulder to shoulder" (34), seeing and hearing nothing, are meant to illustrate the ridiculousness of romantic love.

"Couldst Thou But Know": Edna's Pursuit of the Beloved

Once we are told about their appearance as they enter the pension: "They were leaning toward each other as the water-oaks bent from the sea. There was not a particle of earth beneath their feet" (22). Romance, the image suggests, offers no permanent support, only the temporary brace of dependency. It is significant that Robert, walking toward the ocean in chapter 10, deliberately positions himself between the pair, perhaps envious of their romance, or afraid of falling in love himself, or vaguely aware of the impossibility of romantic love: his motive, "even to himself," is "not wholly clear" (27).

But Chopin repeatedly emphasizes that Edna's feelings for Robert have always been, and will always be, physical. "Romance" is not a separate emotion, only a gentler word for sexual attraction. Edna, for example, lacks an important trait of one typical romantic heroine, Meg March: she never loses her appetite during her romance with Robert. Her hunger represents, in part, the prominence of the sensual and the physical in her life. Also, the explanation she offers Mademoiselle Reisz for her love for Robert is revealing in its quietly ironic and seemingly innocent emphasis on physical detail. Her attraction, clearly, is based on a kind of sentimental chemistry: "Why?" she begins. "Because his hair is brown and grows away from his temples; because he opens and shuts his eyes, and his nose is a little out of drawing; because he has two lips and a square chin, and a little finger which he can't straighten from having played baseball too energetically in his youth. Because—." Mademoiselle has heard enough. "Because you do, in short" (81), she laughs, interrupting Edna and ending her list.

As Emily Toth has disclosed, on 16 January 1898, five days before Chopin completed *The Awakening*, a response of Chopin's to the question "Is Love Divine?" appeared in the *St. Louis Post-Dispatch*. Alluding to Edna's explanation of her love for Robert in her "new novel," Chopin, tellingly, said: "It is as difficult to distinguish between the divine love and the natural, animal love, as it is to explain just why we love at all." She continued, "I am inclined to think that love springs from animal instinct, and therefore is, in a measure, divine. One can never resolve to love this man, this woman or child, and then carry out the resolution unless one feels irresistibly drawn by an indefinable current of magnetism."[7]   The reason for the difficulty of her response, of course, is that two forms of attraction do not exist, but only one.

In the end Edna realizes that "there was no human being whom she wanted near her except Robert; and she even realized that the day would come when he, too, and the thought of him would melt out of her existence, leaving her alone" (113). Edna's courage, and our admiration for her, continue to grow as she moves closer to understanding and wisdom, shedding the false and glittering trappings of romance and "the beloved" in favor of a hard look at the wound that, as we already know through metaphor, will be the "death wound" that ends her life.

8

"I Am Becoming an Artist. Think of It!"

While Edna explores sex and romance as possible sources of fulfillment and happiness, she simultaneously experiments with a third alter-
native to the domestic cult of her day—art. When Mademoiselle Reisz
asks her what she has been doing since her return to New Orleans,
Edna responds, "Painting!" She continues, "I am becoming an artist.
Think of it!" (63). But as we know, however excellent her progress,
Edna does not achieve her goal.

Edna shows signs throughout the novel of truly beginning to
understand what art demands. She learns the meaning of
Mademoiselle Reisz's elusive speech about the artist's "courageous
soul." "What do you mean by the courageous soul?" Edna had once
asked. "Courageous, *ma foi*!" Mademoiselle Reisz responded. "The
brave soul. The soul that dares and defies" (63). We watch Edna coun-
tering nineteenth-century attitudes about artistic women. We admire
her courage, and her difference.

For example, Edna commences her artistic life as a "dabbler"
but soon begins to think of painting as her "work"—a very unconven-
tional notion for a nineteenth-century woman to adopt. Early in the
novel we learn that during one visit to Adèle's on Grand Isle, "Mrs.

Pontellier had brought her sketching materials, which she sometimes dabbled with in an unprofessional way. She liked the dabbling. She felt in it satisfaction of a kind which no other employment afforded her" (13).

At this point painting is, perhaps, only a pseudo-art for Edna, the kind of art great women artists over the centuries have looked upon with deep suspicion and scorn. Anne Finch in her poem "The Spleen" (1701) insists on avoiding the "artistic" options available to women of her time. She will not

> . . . in fading Silks compose
> Faintly th' inimitable *Rose*,
> Fill up an ill-drawn *Bird*, or paint on Glass
> The *Sov'reign's* blurr'd and undistinguish'd Face,
> The threatning *Angel*, and the speaking *Ass*. (147)

In book 1 of Elizabeth Barrett Browning's *Aurora Leigh*, Aurora registers her disdain for the "womanly" education encouraged by her pious aunt, whom we have already seen trying to win Aurora to her cage. Resentfully she recalls, "I danced the polka and Cellarius, / Spun glass, stuffed birds, and modelled flowers in wax, / Because she liked accomplishments in girls." And finally, she writes, "I learnt cross-stitch, because she did not like / To see me wear the night with empty hands, / A-doing nothing" (14–15).

By the time Edna returns home to New Orleans and Esplanade Street, however, her idle interest has become her work. When she shows Adèle some of her sketches, she presents them with the comment, "I believe I ought to work again. I feel as if I wanted to be doing something" (55). She later tells Alcée Arobin, "I've got to work when the weather is bright" (76). Chopin herself is quick to adopt the term to describe what it is Edna is doing in the atelier: "She was working with great energy and interest" (57), Chopin writes.

The idea that art is "work," in both the sense of difficult labor and of one's true vocation, was not prevalent among nineteenth-century women. Adèle's attitude would have been far more common. Madame Ratignolle plays the piano to beautify her home and enrich the lives of her family. "She played very well," we learn, "keeping excellent waltz time and infusing an expression into the strains which was indeed inspiring. She was keeping up her music on account of the children, she said; because she and her husband both considered it a means of brightening the home and making it attractive" (25). The music journalist James Huneker, writing in 1904 about the passing of this type of musician, called her a "piano girl," someone "who devote[s] time to the keyboard merely for the purpose of social display."[1]

Having been given information about Adèle's artistic attitude, we might guess that her selection of the piano as her instrument is significant as a statement of her ingrained assumptions about domestic art. Keyboard instruments, as the editor Carol Neuls-Bates claims in her book *Women in Music* (1982), have since the Renaissance been sex-typed as "feminine." As she points out, keyboard instruments could not only be played at home but also required "no alteration in facial expression or physical demeanor."[2] Of course, selected and played by a true artist, the piano makes no such "feminine" allowances. When Mademoiselle Reisz plays, "her body settled into ungraceful curves and angles that gave it an appearance of deformity" (64).

Adèle's place of practice and performance is also significant. The piano resides in the central living area of her home. Edna practices her art in the atelier, "a bright room in the top of the house" (57). Her art does not inhabit the domestic center. Family and servants who pose for her must make a trip to her private space. Her sons at first enjoy sitting for their portraits but soon lose interest "when they discovered it was not a game arranged especially for their entertainment" (57). It is a little ironic that even the domestic helpers she employs become less attentive to housework when they pose for Edna in her atelier. When the quadroon nanny sits for Edna, the housemaid watches the children and the drawing room goes undusted. Sometimes the housemaid sits, and, no doubt, work below stops altogether when she does. It is more than a little ironic that Léonce, after he chides Edna for her neglect of "the comfort of her family" by retreating so often to the atelier, goes "away to his office" (57). He fails to recognize the irony of having, and needing, his own private retreat from domestic activity and demands while scolding his wife for needing hers.

Not surprisingly, Léonce once declared his admiration for Adèle's brand of music and art, for her ability to see art as a sweet supplement to family life.[3] Arguing with Edna about the disproportionate amount of time she has been devoting to her painting, he holds Adèle up as a model. Léonce pronounces as "utmost folly" Edna's habit of spending "in an atelier days which would be better employed contriving for the comfort of her family" (57). And he finds proof: "There's Madame Ratignolle; because she keeps up her music, she doesn't let everything else go to chaos" (57).

Germaine Greer, writing about female painters in the nineteenth century in *The Obstacle Race: The Fortunes of Women Painters and Their Work* (1979), reminds us that most women of the century viewed their talent as "genteel accomplishment" and "pleasant pastime." Though many women were forced into aggressively pursuing their talent owing to financial necessity, Greer assures us that "few of them believed that the practice of art was in itself superior to a life of wedded bliss."[4]

Mary Kelley makes a similar observation about American women writers of the period. Female writers often entered the arena of popular sentimental fiction only out of financial necessity. This was true of Sara Parton, Maria McIntosh, E. D. E. N. Southworth, and Susan Warner. Kelley reminds us that in nineteenth-century America "nine out of ten women married, and for the large majority of them the household remained the locus of occupation" (143). Kelley refers to the words of warning and advice Sara Parton's character Ruth Hall gives to her daughter: "No happy woman ever writes" (138). Kelley concludes, "The female vocation, then, was domesticity, in colonial as well as in independent America" (141). Adèle's attitude toward art, not Edna's—and most certainly not Mademoiselle Reisz's—was socially correct.

As Edna awakens personally, and as she develops a greater commitment to art, she begins to paint in a more original way. We cannot help but associate her progress with Chopin's own. In 1890 Chopin wrote a very conventional first novel, *At Fault*; it contains not only neat resolutions and fairly traditional notions of plot and subplot, but two parts divided into 12 and 17 chapters, respectively, with titles like

"The Self-Assumed Burden" and "A Step Too Far." Nine years later Chopin would produce *The Awakening*—not only a shorter novel, with 39 chapters of highly irregular length, but one of great lyrical and impressionistic intensity. Sandra Gilbert proposes that *The Awakening*, with "its odd short chapters, its ambiguous lyricism (what Cather called its 'flexible iridescent style'), its editorial restraint, its use of recurrent images and refrains, its implicit and explicit allusions to writers like Whitman, Swinburne, Flaubert, and its air of moral indeterminacy," demonstrates that Chopin "was working in a mode of mingled naturalism and symbolism exactly analogous to the one explored by her near contemporary George Moore and his younger countryman James Joyce" (45–46).

Edna's subject matter and her style both change. As she experiences more of life and more of art, she moves away from imitation and toward a style of her own. Early on Edna is highly representational—and wants to be. She is annoyed by her inability to copy what is before her exactly and precisely. She has tried to capture Adèle Ratignolle on canvas, the woman seated before her "like some sensuous Madonna, with the gleam of the fading day enriching her splendid color" (13).[5] But Edna, perhaps not yet awakened fully enough to the idea of sensuality in her own nature to capture it in someone else, perhaps not sufficiently confident in her own imagination, or perhaps—in her symbolic role, as Patricia Lattin suggests, as "an anomaly in nineteenth-century Creole society"—never able to copy the mother-woman image, never able to get it quite right (1978, 10), destroys what she has created. "The picture completed bore no resemblance to Madame Ratignolle. She was greatly disappointed to find that it did not look like her" (13), writes Chopin. She smudges her sketch with paint and crumples up the paper in her hands.

But we are allowed to see something that Edna is not yet ready to observe. In spite of the picture's inexactness as a copy of real life, "it was a fair enough piece of work, and in many respects satisfying" (13). We are perhaps not encouraged to respond as enthusiastically as Robert does—*"Mais ce n'est pas mal! Elle s'y connait, elle a de la force, oui"* (Not bad at all! She knows what she's doing, she has talent)—but we are meant to understand that something she possesses other than her capacity for imitation will make Edna's work "satisfying."

How realistically things are copied onto canvas is, appropriately, the standard Adèle uses when she sorts through numerous sketches of Edna's in New Orleans. She calls Edna's talent "immense" and then chooses a favorite: a still life of a basket of apples. Her description of it reveals Adèle's philosophy of artistic "immensity": "and this basket of apples! never have I seen anything more lifelike. One might almost be tempted to reach out a hand and take one" (56).

Edna's growing sensitivity to sensual experience in part leads to her development of a more unique visual sense. Edna, of course, has always been keenly observant: Chopin routinely talks about what she "looks at," "notices," or "sees." But Edna observes somewhat differently after her important summer on Grand Isle. The mental pictures that come to Edna early in the summer as she listens to Madame Ratignolle play reflect the generally more conventional nature of her visual imagination before it is touched by deep sensual awareness. Although one piece anticipates the repressed sensuality that she will recover and incorporate into her art—the picture of a naked man standing desolate by a rock as a bird wings its way heavenward—most of her early images are conventional, proper, and "typical" of the work of nineteenth-century female artists. Michael Gilmore believes that her growing fondness for "imageless" music like Mademoiselle Reisz's reflects the development of a modern consciousness. "An imageless art is autonomous," he writes, "neither mirroring nor duplicating an external form, and it shakes Edna to the depths because it provides immediate entrance to the subjective world of feelings" (78).

Greer writes that "most [nineteenth-century female painters and sculptors] accepted the idea that truly female art was feminine, delicate, dainty, small and soft-voiced, and concerned itself with intimate domestic scenes, especially mothers and children" (321). Three of the early images Edna forms are in line with this understanding and philosophy: one piece reminds Edna of "a dainty young woman clad in an Empire gown, taking mincing dancing steps as she came down a long avenue between tall hedges"; another, we are told, "reminded her of children at play, and still another of nothing on earth but a demure lady stroking a cat" (27).

But after the moonlight swim, after the hours spent with Robert on the Chênière Caminada, after encounters in New Orleans with Alcée Arobin, Edna seems to be ready to see, and to paint, with a more sensual and original touch. Perhaps this is what she knows, or is beginning to know, when she says to the sensuous Adèle in chapter 18, "Perhaps I shall be able to paint your picture some day" (55). She chooses sensuous models. She deliberately summons the housemaid, having "perceived that the young woman's back and shoulders were molded on classic lines, and that her hair, loosened from its confining cap, became an inspiration" (58).

Edna's pursuit of more original and serious art is directly linked to her development of greater self-pride and confidence, as well as to the emergence of her sensuality. The more she paints, the more confident she becomes in herself and in her work. She always remains critical of her canvases, as an artist must, but not in the destructive way we see early in the novel. When Edna tears up her sketch of Madame Ratignolle, her gesture is almost one of self-loathing; her smudging and crumpling of her work remind us of a child being shamed by a parent.

Before studying with Laidpore, Edna has little genuine trust in her talent. Looking over sketches to show Adèle, we learn that "she could see their shortcomings and defects, which were glaring in her eyes" (54). And when Léonce scolds her for spending more time with her paints than with her children, she quickly admits, "[Adèle] isn't a musician, and I'm not a painter" (57). She continues to work after this upbraiding "with great energy and interest, without accomplishing anything, however, which satisfied her even in the smallest degree" (57).

We are glad that Edna is self-demanding, glad to know that her expectations are high and her standards unyielding. But what we sense as we watch her is that, unfortunately, the criticism hurled at her throughout her life—by her father, her sister Margaret, Léonce—has been deeply absorbed and integrated into her self-concept. And although her mother's death has provided her with a small inheritance and an important beginning of a connection with the woman who bore her, Edna must recover her mother's memory more fully if she is ever to understand how to form loving connections with the rest of the world. It is interesting that Chopin treats Edna's motherlessness so briefly and, apparently, so casually. Edna's avoidance of the issue suggests how painful it is. We know that her mother died when Edna and her sisters were young, but probably not before they witnessed their father's abusiveness and brutality toward his wife. The silence about Edna's mother speaks loudly, for it confirms our suspicion that Edna knows all too well what we are told about her parents: "He had coerced his own wife into her grave" (71). The silence also forces us to wonder if Edna's mother might also have chosen to kill herself. What more convincing reason could there have been than the nineteenth-century shame of suicide to keep her name from the lips of her own family? How might "coerce . . . into her grave" be better read?

Edna's confidence does grow during the months we know her. Even though she seeks Madame Ratignolle's opinion about whether to study art, we are told very directly that Edna has already made up her mind on this point. "She knew that Madame Ratignolle's opinion in such a matter would be next to valueless, that she herself had not alone decided, but determined" (55). We are told at the start of chapter 25 that "she had reached a stage when she seemed to be no longer feeling her way, working, when in the humor, with sureness and ease" (73). Summarizing her progress for Mademoiselle Reisz in chapter 26, Edna talks about both her teacher's response to her work and her own more positive assessments of her progress: "Laidpore is more and more pleased with my work; he says it grows in force and individuality. I cannot judge of that myself, but I feel that I have gained in ease and confidence" (79). And as we have seen earlier, the fact that her painting is beginning to see a profit pleases Edna. One of the last visits she makes is with a picture dealer who wishes to hire her to complete some Parisian scenes for the December Christmas trade should she go to France to study.

The last picture we hear about, a "character study" of "a young Italian" (94), which she had been working on before she pays a visit to

Mademoiselle Reisz—and is unexpectedly reunited with Robert—unfortunately must remain a mystery to us. But that is perhaps exactly where it belongs, exactly what Chopin intended. We can imagine from the abbreviated descriptions Chopin provides, and from her earlier record of Edna's growing attraction to physical texture and form, that the model was appealing in some profoundly sensual way. We also find clues in being told that Edna is working with greater confidence in a nonrepresentational form. For example, Edna has worked on this study all morning "without the model" (94), entirely from her imagination, in marked contrast to her earlier insistence on copying what is before her.

But why, if Edna's painting is growing in confidence, originality, and sensuality, does she not succeed in becoming an artist? What is it that holds her back?

Edna, unlike some other artists in Chopin's canon, fears solitude. It is not until the very last scene of the book that she is able to admit that she is "absolutely alone" (113)—words, as we will see, that Chopin introduces in a highly significant way. Until she can embrace the fact of solitude, Edna cannot be an artist. By the time she does, it is too late.

Chopin's true artists—Mademoiselle Reisz in *The Awakening* and Paula Von Stoltz in her early story "Wiser Than a God" (1889)[6] are willing to live with the thought of being alone, with only art as their true companion. Edna is not. All three women, we are to believe, have the natural talent of the artist. Mademoiselle Reisz plays with "abiding truth" (27); Paula has both technical skill and "the touch and interpretation of the artist" ("Wiser," 43) when she seats herself at the piano; and Edna, we learn, handles her brushes "with a certain ease and freedom which came, not from long and close acquaintance with them, but from a natural aptitude" (13).

But Mademoiselle Reisz has warned Edna that natural talent, no matter how great, is not sufficient. An artist must also have, we remember, "the courageous soul" (63). One must have not only talent but temperament, Mademoiselle Reisz has cautioned. And a major component of artistic temperament, as both Paula Von Stoltz and Mademoiselle Reisz demonstrate through their own examples, is the ability to live alone. Mademoiselle Reisz, unlike Edna, reserves the status of "beloved" for her piano, her "beloved instrument" (80). Solitude and art are inseparable companions. Perhaps this is what Edna finds so difficult to understand when she says about Mademoiselle Reisz, "I only half comprehend her" (83).

Paula Von Stoltz tries, sometimes tearfully, to explain her decision to live alone with art to George Brainard, the man who adores and pursues her. "I can't marry you," she explains, painfully, "because it doesn't enter into the purpose of my life." She continues, "Can't you feel that with me, it courses with the blood through my veins? That it's something dearer than life, than riches, even than love?" Having made her vow to art, she compares herself to a nun in a convent. George can only respond, "Paula listen to me; don't speak like a mad woman" ("Wiser," 46). She becomes a renowned concert pianist, a rare accomplishment for a woman in the nineteenth century.[7]

There is little doubt that Paula has made the correct decision. George Brainard is described to us at the end of the story, many years later, with mild mockery. We understand what Paula's life might have been like had she married him, and we are relieved that she did not. We are glad she is in Leipzig on an "extended and remunerative concert tour." "George Brainard is as handsome as ever," Chopin concludes, "though growing a little stout in the quiet routine of domestic life. He has quite lost a pretty taste for music that formerly distinguished him as a skilful banjoist. This loss his little black-eyed wife deplores; though she has herself made concessions to the advancing years, and abandoned Virginia break-downs as incompatible with the serious offices of wifehood and matrimony" ("Wiser," 47).

Chopin attaches to her story a final sentence for conventional readers, indicating that Paula may later marry her harmony teacher, but it is a totally unconvincing touch. We know that solitude, not love, has brought Paula's genius to the foreground.

Through Chopin's portrait of Mademoiselle Reisz, we are shown that solitude was not an easy, comfortable, or conventionally appealing option for a nineteenth-century woman. Mademoiselle Reisz is associated repeatedly with black lace and violets, a flower that John Vickery notes has been connected to "rites of protection against harm" by Sir James Frazer.[8] For a nineteenth-century woman to be as alone as she is—to not rely on a man for support and sustenance—is a terrible risk. In some strange way, the violets protect and comfort her, and she is dependent on them. She has become quarrelsome, wizened, and disagreeable through the effort of maintaining her independence and assertiveness. Many think her mad. Arobin conveys the community's consensus when he explains to Edna, "I've heard she's partially demented" (83). His words echo George Brainard's assessment of Paula Von Stoltz in 1889 and link Chopin with the traditional literature about madness in women.[9]

But Edna's response to Arobin's comment is meant to be the correct one. She says that Mademoiselle Reisz "seems to me wonderfully sane" (83). In spite of the personal price that solitude has made her pay, Mademoiselle Reisz is the center of beauty in the novel: her first chords send "a keen tremor down Mrs. Pontellier's spinal column" because they sound "the abiding truth" (27). And she is the center of wisdom. Her speeches fill Edna with wonder. Important phrases and fragments from them are repeated in the final pages for us to remember.

It is true that Edna, like Chopin's two great artists, hates many kinds of interruptions that call her away from her work. She visits Mademoiselle Reisz in chapter 33 largely because of her annoyance with "many interruptions, some incident to her modest housekeeping, and others of a social nature" (94)—primarily the visits of Madame Ratignolle, Mrs. Merriman, and Mrs. Highcamp. But Edna, we must recognize, often chooses to allow rather empty social commitments to interrupt her work. Her temperament, in spite of her great strides toward independence and her embrace of the new concept of supportive female friendship that Mademoiselle Reisz has begun to teach her, remains, in some essential ways, socially conventional and dependent.

It must be remembered that Edna's time and social climate offered many quiet rewards to women for self-abnegation and dependency. Jo March in *Little Women* loses artistic heart because she finally cannot resist the message conveyed to females in countless ways that unmarried and unloved women are somehow pathetic. She cannot defy the idea that producing books, inanimate objects, is inferior to producing children and happy homes. Jo, almost 25 years old, fears the worst before Mr. Bhaer rescues her: "An old maid, that's what I'm to be. A literary spinster, with a pen for a spouse, a family of stories for children, and twenty years hence a morsel of fame, perhaps; when, like poor Johnson, I'm old, and can't enjoy it, solitary, and can't share it, independent, and don't need it" (489–90). Even Aurora Leigh disappoints us when, in book 9, she chooses Romney after suddenly realizing, "Art is much, but love is more" (341).

Part of Edna's unhealthy dependency also seems to come from the unsupportive childhood we have already mentioned. She had no mother, feared her severe father, was ruled by her practical and matronly sister Margaret, quarreled with her sister Janet, and found it difficult to form emotional friendships with girlfriends. Elizabeth Fox-Genovese, echoing the sentiments of Ruth Smith and Stewart Sullivan in their 1973 work on Chopin, believes that Edna's motherlessness cannot be overstated, that it "lies at the core of *The Awakening*."[10]

Edna's dependency intrudes on her work in many forms. Once, we are told, desire for Robert interrupts her effort. "A subtle current of desire passed through her body, weakening her hold upon the brushes and making her eyes burn" (58), Chopin explains. Edna's failure to be self-reliant, as George Arms notes, is anticipated in Chopin's image of her falling asleep while reading Emerson. Her sleepiness reading the transcendentalist, Arms feels, "hints that Edna's individualism lacks philosophical grounding" (219) and helps define the irony implicit in the book's title. But we can also find in the image information about one particular source of her artistic failure: sleep is the place where dreams occur, and dreams of Robert are what Edna craves.

Edna also cannot resist being with Alcée, even though she is haunted by dreams of artistic neglect. In an extremely odd dream, she pictures Mr. Highcamp playing the piano at the entrance to a Canal Street music store. While he is playing, his wife boards an Esplanade Street streetcar with Alcée and says, "What a pity that so much talent has been neglected! but I must go" (75). Edna herself accompanies Alcée to the races a few days after her dream. But she attempts to correct the pleasure and excitement of the day with her evening vow not to neglect her work by going to the races with Alcée again. Her vow echoes the guilt her earlier dream of Mr. Highcamp seems to have inspired and made clear: "No . . . I've had enough of the races. I don't want to lose all the money I've won, and I've got to work when the weather is bright, instead of—" (76). She breaks her vow very quickly, however, as her intimacy with Alcée grows, first "by imperceptible degrees, and then by leaps" (78).

Edna's relationships with women are also often influenced by her former emotional deprivation and her susceptibility to conventional notions of friendships among women. Edna looks too often to receive quick approval and affection rather than to form relationships that will deeply sustain and allow growth. She gathers her sketches in her arms to show to Madame Ratignolle, knowing from the start of her trip to her friend's house how worthless Adèle's words and opinions will be; nonetheless, "she sought the words and praise and encouragement that would help her to put heart into her venture" (55). Adèle's praise, we are told, makes Edna feel complacent, an emotion that retards rather than inspires work and can never be the core of true art—or true friendship.

Through the character of Mademoiselle Reisz, Chopin introduces Edna to the possibility of a more vital and sustaining form of friendship between women than she has known before. Although Mademoiselle Reisz is not as flattering as Adèle, her concern for Edna is clearly more genuine and more constructive. She forces Edna to see the truth about Victor and Robert, about romantic infatuation, about art, and about female courage. Edna simultaneously loves and fears Mademoiselle Reisz. She is beginning to distinguish between the conventional support of women like Adèle and the more radical, bold support of a Mademoiselle Reisz, but flattery continues to entice her at times.

Willa Cather, in her 1899 review of *The Awakening*, made an important comment on the place of art in women's lives, even though, ironically, her review registered only a limited understanding of Edna's suicide and never indicated that Cather was aware of Edna's desire to paint. She called fanciful idealists and romantics like Edna the "Bovary type" and said of them: "These people really expect the passion of love to fill and gratify every need of life, whereas nature only intended it should meet one of many demands. They insist upon making it stand for all the emotional pleasures of life and art; expecting an individual and self-limited passion to yield infinite variety, pleasure, and distraction, to contribute to their lives what the arts and the pleasurable exercise of the intellect gives to less limited and less intense idealists."[11] The content and tone of Cather's remarks bring to mind the bust of Beethoven in *The Awakening* that, "covered with a hood of dust, scowled at [Edna] from the mantelpiece" (78). Cather's remarks also explain the mysterious final sneer from Mademoiselle Reisz that Edna imagines as she walks into the Gulf.

But are *we* to sneer at Edna as well? On the one hand, she does seem unable to concentrate on her art as she must, unable to face solitude, unable to live without the flattery of attractive men and of complacent women, unable to form and embrace relationships that might complement rather than hinder her personal and artistic growth. On the other hand, Edna makes great progress in her understanding of herself as an artist, growing more confident, more original, more committed. Are we really going to insist on an ideal standard for Edna and ignore her progress? Does she have to complete her journey for us to find her commendable?

Is Chopin, perhaps, testing the very way we have traditionally approached and judged fictional characters—and art itself? Is she quietly suggesting that traditional assumptions about art and the artist must be questioned by the modern consciousness about to emerge? Patricia Lattin notes that in many ways *The Awakening* is harmonious with the late twentieth century, for it avoids easy resolutions and implies "that achieving selfhood is difficult, sometimes even impossible."[12] Marianne Hirsch and Susan Rosowski have strongly suggested that the novel of awakening is decidedly different from the traditional bildungsroman.

To the very last moment of her life Edna makes progress toward acquiring the virtues artists must have, even though her journey is never completed. As we have begun to hint and will further examine, Edna is finally able to face solitude at the end of her life. She is learning to understand and appreciate her supportive friendship with

Mademoiselle Reisz. She has been able to renounce her dependency on Alcée, Léonce, and even Robert. After reading her concluding thoughts, we might wonder why these new strengths, the strengths of the artist, do not give her courage to turn toward shore and all the canvases yet unpainted. But the book's final pages disclose clearly a final insurmountable barrier to her art—and to her life.

9

Understanding Edna's Suicide

The St. Louis World's Fair of 1904 was written about exuberantly in many of the nation's popular magazines. In September 1904, for example, John Brisben Walker prepared a special 144-page issue on the World's Fair for *Cosmopolitan*. In a section entitled "Woman's Progress since the World's Fair at Chicago" Walker listed six indicators of women's advancement since 1893. Household inventions such as convenient dust-removing devices were featured and applauded, as were books that systematically compiled domestic information. The most telling of the six items, however, was the fourth: "The acceptance of motherhood as a profession, requiring thorough recognition of the fact that it brings woman's highest reward."[1]

Maternal—not human—dignity was the goal the nineteenth century urged women to attain. But Edna, we have already seen, "was beginning to realize her position in the universe as a human being, and to recognize her relations as an individual to the world within and about her" (14–15). Edna senses, even in the earliest stages of her awakening, that a woman's identity as a human being is more important and essential (and certainly more sacred) than her role as a mother. She once tells Madame Ratignolle, "I would give up the unessential; I would give my money, I would give my life for my children; but I wouldn't give myself. I can't make it more clear; it's only something which I am beginning to comprehend, which is revealing itself to me" (48).

Although Edna is never much more articulate than this about the central place of individual human importance in her life, her final act—her suicide—dramatizes her mysterious understanding of a revolutionary concept of gender: women must be given "thorough recognition" because of their worth as human beings, not because of their reproductive capability. Edna, of course, never attains the full "human" status she seeks. But in refusing to live without it, refusing to yield to the philosophy of motherhood that informed and directed her age, she ironically is reborn and, in a sense, gives birth to greater human possibility for women in the century to come.

Appropriately, it is the issue of motherhood that dominates the book's final pages and chapters. Priscilla Allen, annoyed by critical interpretations that have neglected the role of children in Edna's final act, writes, "One wonders how [critics] can explain Chopin's placing of the birth scene—or the inclusion of it at all—in the story, especially in a novel so artfully and economically structured" (237). Allen feels that ignoring this scene has led critics to make "a soap-opera of the novel's ending" (236) because they can only see Edna's despair as a direct consequence of her abandonment by Robert Lebrun. Indeed, critics from Cather to Spangler to Showalter to Lupton have all at one time done just this.[2]

It is the issue of motherhood, perhaps more than anything else, that forces Edna into the sea. She sees no way for a mother to keep the freedom of her soul—no way, that is, except to dissolve her attachment to her children.

It is not surprising that Edna's shirking of her maternal duty was a prime target of Chopin's contemporary reviewers. The reviewer for the *New Orleans Times-Democrat*, for example, saw Edna as a woman so absorbed in her personal relation to her own world that she "fails to perceive that the relation of a mother to her children is far more important than the gratification of a passion."[3] Priscilla Allen, however, points out something even more deeply disturbing. Edna was chastised for being an irresponsible mother not only by early critics but also by later ones. Allen writes, "Modern critics are also surprisingly similar to the turn-of-the-century critics in their judgments of Edna's 'failure to her duty' as wife and mother. This is a negative way to approach Edna's real and important actions—to emphasize what she doesn't do instead of focussing on her real accomplishments" (227). Just a few hours before her death, after witnessing Adèle's childbirth, Edna pleads with Dr. Mandelet, "Don't blame me for anything" (110). But it has taken critics—and, perhaps, our century—far too long to honor her request.

The nineteenth century's message of the supremacy of motherhood was so strong and so intense that it was absorbed into the systems of its women—even women like Edna who were not maternally inclined. Significantly, through Chopin's decision to make Edna rich, we are assured that Edna's abandonment of her children is founded not on selfish whim but, rather, on a deep and profound philosophical complaint. At first, we misread the role Edna's wealth plays in the story. We judge her more severely than we might otherwise precisely because she seems to have so few real maternal demands placed on her. Why should we believe Edna's claim that motherhood has enslaved her soul? How much credibility can such a plea have when it comes from a character who can afford a quadroon maid to baby-sit full-time and to play croquet with the children under the live oaks while she swims with her lover in the sea? From a character whose mother-in-law greedily and lovingly keeps her grandsons in the country for weeks and months at a time? If Edna had been physically devastated by the job of rearing her children, a single urban mother perhaps, we could better understand her intense desire to escape the responsibilities of her small boys. Edna annoys us at first because she seems to have so little to do and so much leisure. What *is* she complaining about anyway?

Chopin forces the question and in the process forces us to see the truly radical nature of her novel. Edna senses the true cause of the millions of practical complaints about motherhood that other women have uttered. Chopin, by increasing our annoyance with Edna's leisured brand of motherhood, forces us to sense it, too. It is clearly not just the duties of motherhood that are oppressive but the very concept of motherhood itself. More oppressive than the daily demands of children is the century's pervasive and limiting notion of gender, the notion that a woman's duty and reward are found in motherhood. Edna, though strikingly different from most women of her century—she is never a "mother-woman" like Adèle—cannot avoid her age's inescapable perception of women as dutiful mothers, except in death. Society, as well as the conscience of Edna herself, offers no relief.

Edna's deep ambivalence, caused in large part by her natural inheritance of her century's philosophy, prohibits her from resolving her dilemma. Her confusion is clear during her final conversation with Dr. Mandelet. As the words of Adèle linger in her memory ("Think of the children, Edna. Oh think of the children! Remember them!" [109]), she voices the tension in her heart in incoherent, clipped remarks. "I'm not going to be forced into doing things. I don't want to go abroad. I want to be let alone. Nobody has any right—except children, perhaps—and even then, it seems to me—or it did seem—" (109).

The book's final paragraphs continue to connect Edna's last act more strongly with irresolvable issues of children and motherhood than with other matters. The night after Robert leaves her, Edna thinks about many of the disappointments in her life, but with relative indifference. "To-day it is Arobin; to-morrow it will be some one else. It makes no difference to me, it doesn't matter about Léonce Pontellier." Edna's mood shifts, however, when the thought of her sons intrudes. After the dash, Chopin writes, "but Raoul and Etienne!" (113). She is disturbed rather than tranquil. We are next told, "She understood now clearly what she had meant long ago when she said to Adèle Ratignolle that she would give up the unessential, but she would never sacrifice herself for her children" (113). Motherhood and selfhood were incompatible in Edna's century, and in some ways, as we have seen, incompatible in Edna herself. Even if children and motherhood are, as Dr. Mandelet tries to explain to Edna, "arbitrary conditions which we create, and which we feel obliged to maintain at any cost" (110), the moral implications of her role are so deeply a part of Edna's psyche that there is no way to remove them, except through death.

As Chopin continues to record Edna's thoughts the night before
her suicide, we learn of other things that no longer matter to her. The
language, again, at first is calm and indifferent, rational, factual, and
decisive. "There was no one thing in the world that she desired," we
are told. "There was no human being whom she wanted near her
except Robert" (113). The construction of both sentences is weak and
unemphatic, complementing Edna's minimal concern. Very analytical-
ly, we are then told that Edna "realized" (113) she would one day not
even desire Robert. But in this paragraph, as in the one before, the
thought of the children next intrudes, at which point the language
once again becomes dramatic, punctuated by strong nouns and verbs,
military and oppressive. "The children appeared before her like antagonists who had overcome her; who had overpowered and sought to
drag her into the soul's slavery for the rest of her days" (113). Then
Edna's plan is hinted at: "But she knew a way to elude them" (113).
The conjunction here is between the children and the act of suicide;
Edna is not thinking of Robert when she thinks of "them."

Edna's immediate thoughts clarify the source of her despair one
final time. Close to death, now physically exhausted, she remembers
her family. "She thought of Léonce and the children. They were a part
of her life. But they need not have thought that they could possess her,
body and soul" (114). In life, this is exactly what they would have
thought, or, more precisely, what they simply would have assumed.
Ironically, it is also what Edna herself could not have helped thinking
sometimes.

The final sentence of the book symbolically reminds us once
again of the innocent oppression of children, the trait that causes them
to loom as "antagonists" in Edna's mind. All the images of the final
paragraph are images of oppression—the voices of Edna's father and
matronly sister Margaret, the barking of a dog that is chained by its
master, the spurs of a cavalry officer that can wound and bring obedience. Then, quietly, the book ends with what appears to be a gentle
glimpse of nature: "There was the hum of bees, and the musky odor of
pinks filled the air" (114).

But as gentle and decorative as the line seems, we must remember what, after all, is occurring. *Musk*, of course, is a word that

invites sexual associations.[4] Fertilization is going on right before our eyes. Elaine Showalter observes that the image of bees pollinating flowers fits securely within the tradition of writing by American women, "where it is a standard trope for the unequal sexual relations between women and men" (53). Showalter supports her historical observation by quoting from the journal of the nineteenth-century feminist writer Margaret Fuller: "Woman is the flower, man the bee. She sighs out of melodious fragrance, and invites the winged laborer. He drains her cup, and carries off the honey. She dies on the stalk; he returns to the hive, well fed, and praised as an active member of the community."[5] Chopin, unlike Fuller, offers no interpretation of her final image. But if we find it pretty, or even neutral, we had better look again.

Edna refuses to return to a world that values only her performance as a mother, whose highest expectations for women are self-sacrifice and self-effacement. She refuses to return to a world in which this idea is pervasive and inescapable—and unavoidably colors even her own thinking. For Edna, there is, ideally, a truth greater than that of motherhood. Motherhood, compared with it, becomes yet another illusion that Edna must dispel. That final truth, that greater truth, cannot coexist with the social, the moral, or even the biological obligations of motherhood.

To a great extent, motherhood also prevents Edna from successfully translating this higher truth into a life of artistic pursuit and endeavor. We may argue that Edna fails as an artist simply because she is less courageous than her mentor, less sure of herself, less bold and independent. But we also must consider a very important difference between the two (a difference, we recall, that Seyersted noticed generally between Edna and other heroines of major turn-of-the-century novels): Mademoiselle Reisz is childless. It is important to remember that until very recently most serious women artists have been childless. Critics of women's literature have often noted that most of the greatest female writers have not borne children. The contemporary poet Mary Jo Salter recently reminded readers of this telling and sad fact in a comprehensive essay on women poets. "Most women writers of fiction in history have been childless," she states. "The list of the best women poets in our language . . . is a nearly unbroken catalog of child-lessness: Elizabeth Barrett Browning (who had one child, late), Emily Dickinson, Christina Rossetti, Charlotte Mew, Marianne Moore, Louise Bogan, Elizabeth Bishop, May Swenson, etc. etc." She adds, in a darkly humorous fashion, "If we take comfort in remembering that Sylvia Plath was a mother, it is not for long: we know what happened to her."[6]

Edna does not even consider art an option in the thoughts that conclude the book. She is obsessed, rather, by the issue of mother-hood—the very issue that the majority of female artists in the nine-teenth century avoided (at whatever personal cost) by remaining childless. The issue is so enormous, so consuming, so historically irrec-oncilable with female artistic talent and ambition that it seems perfect-ly correct that Edna would forget her brushes on the final afternoon of her life. After studying the theme of motherhood throughout Chopin's canon, Patricia Lattin, as we have seen, concludes that in her fiction having children "generally proves disastrous, causing insanity, death, and—of most significance to Chopin—a woman's loss of self." Lattin feels that "although Chopin never openly crusaded against the injus-tices of her time, her presentation of childbirth and motherhood makes clear that she thought nineteenth-century America limited human possibilities" (1978, 12).

Throughout the novel Edna defies what is not true. Eventually we see that what she most defies is the central perception of her centu-ry that women are mothers first and individuals second—or not at all. She never denies the value of motherhood and admits on more than one occasion that the children "were a part of her life." But she does deny its supremacy over larger truths of human existence.

Edna, it is true, never learns all that she might about her human-ity and its potential. She leaves the world too soon for that. But she makes a good beginning toward self-discovery, and she shows us—as well as the century that follows hers—much about the process. She has, as we have seen, freed herself of illusions about marriage, domes-ticity, and nineteenth-century womanhood. She has also freed herself of the guilt so commonly associated with sexual seduction in sentimental novels of the nineteenth century. In *The Sentimental Novel in America 1789–1860* (1940), Herbert Ross Brown asserts that "of all the causes of suicide in our early fiction, seduction was by far the most powerful." He further explains, "The heroine whose sensibility exceeded her prudence found in suicide a ready escape from the shame, if not the sin, of seduction."[7] The shame of seduction, clearly, is not what causes Edna to kill herself.

We have also seen that she comes to terms with the illusive and insubstantial nature of romantic love by the time the book ends. At best, her love for Robert is only temporary. It will end. And she chooses, in the only way she knows how, to free herself of the illusion of motherhood. After shedding lies and half-truths, Edna embraces the truth she chooses to die with (or, perhaps, die *for*): the self must be preserved and honored and loved. As Edna so rightly senses, and her critics so wrongly sensed, self-love is not the same as selfish love. She would begin to discover and love what made her human—and to celebrate it.

Chopin originally entitled her novel *A Solitary Soul*. Margaret Culley implies that the title Chopin chose correctly highlights the "many brave moments of delight she takes in her solitary self" ("Edna," 228). Emily Toth suggests a connection between Chopin's title and her intention of making the book "a hymn to aloneness as a source of strength and power" (1990, 21).

One of the important discoveries Edna makes is that solitude and selfhood are deeply connected, a principle that radically challenged the public, domestic image of women in the nineteenth century. In A. S. Byatt's expansive and polyphonic novel about both the nineteenth and twentieth centuries, *Possession* (1990), the fictitious nineteenth-century poet Christabel LaMotte addresses the issue of solitude in women's lives. Solitude, she writes, thinking of legends and fairy tales, "is a thing we women are taught to dread—oh the terrible tower, oh the thickets round it—no companionable Nest—but a donjon." "But," Christabel continues, "they have lied to us you know . . . my Solitude is my Treasure, the best thing I have."[8]

Ralph Waldo Emerson, a writer both Chopin and her character Edna knew, talks about the essential matter of solitude in "Self-

Reliance" (1841), which may be the essay Edna was reading after her return from Grand Isle. "The great man is he who in the midst of the crowd keeps with perfect sweetness the independence of solitude," he writes.[9] Emerson understands in "The Transcendentalist" (1842) that society looks on those who choose a "solitary and critical way of living" as selfish, indolent, and unfit, exactly the assessment of Edna's acquaintances and family—as well as her early readers. Emerson imagines the societal response that Edna would experience: "It saith, Whoso goes to walk alone, accuses the whole world; he declareth all to be unfit to be his companions; it is very uncivil, nay, insulting; Society will retaliate." But Emerson understands and encourages the need for solitude in people like Edna Pontellier. He continues, "Meantime, this retirement does not proceed from any whim on the part of these separators; but if any one will take pains to talk with them, he will find that this part is chosen both from temperament and from principle; with some unwillingness, too."[10]

Like Emerson's man of solitude, Edna is often "unwilling" to become the solitary soul she is inclined to be by both temperament and principle. Although she is frequently attracted to contemplative moments of privacy and solitude, Edna is not willing to be "absolutely alone" until the close of the novel. Throughout the nine months we know her, she needs the admiration and attention of lovers, seeks the easy approval of women friends like Adèle Ratignolle, and fails to pursue as aggressively as she might more difficult but sustaining relationships with characters such as Mademoiselle Reisz and Dr. Mandelet, relationships that would complement artistic solitude rather than impair it. She also suffers from the universal fear we all have of facing alone a sometimes very frightening existential world, a world that resembles "a grotesque pandemonium" and in which human beings sometimes look "like worms struggling blindly toward inevitable annihilation" (58).

Only at the end of the novel does Edna find the courage to accept and acknowledge her solitary state, the courage to be "absolutely alone" (113). For one brief moment she faces the liberating and frightening vision of complete independence. And in that vision Edna discovers the beginning of truth. Dorothy Goldman suggests that the register of Edna's thoughts at the end demonstrates her "ability progressively to cut herself free from the narrator and become the first person singular."[11] Her solitude, even in terms of Chopin's narrative technique, is absolute.

Chopin prepares us to understand not only Edna's new independence but also her courage, joy, and immense sense of possible connection with her world: a scene in chapter 39 is strongly paralleled by the earlier scene of the moonlight swim in chapter 10. Here Chopin provides us with clues about how to read her book's final sequence.

In the earlier chapter Chopin makes it clear that the acceptance of solitude, represented by the image of the lone swimmer, is an important part of Edna's growth. We are told that Edna had spent the summer learning how to swim. Men, women, and even children in the community had expended significant energy trying to instruct her. And Robert, we are told, "was nearly at the point of discouragement in realizing the futility of his efforts" (28). It is clear from Chopin's continued explanation, however, that Edna's lack of success is linked more strongly to her fear of being alone in water than to her physical limitations. "A certain ungovernable dread hung about her when in the water, unless there was a hand near by that might reach out and reassure her" (28). A reassuring hand, after all, is what she knows she must relinquish to swim. On this moonlit night, when she first gathers the courage to try, she feels like a child who "walks for the first time alone" (28).

The Edna of chapter 10 may be starting to acknowledge her solitary state, but she cannot resist looking back to the secure shore. For a time she turns her head toward the sea, gathering "an impression of space and solitude," of "the unlimited" (29). But then she shifts her glance toward the shore and, significantly, toward the people there who have given her support and reassurance. Soon after this glance back she loses courage. "She had not gone any great distance—that is, what would have been a great distance for an experienced swimmer. But to her unaccustomed vision the stretch of water behind her assumed the aspect of a barrier which her unaided strength would never be able to overcome" (29).

The concept of the independent romantic sea and the dependent slavish shore was one that Chopin was certainly as familiar with as were the major romantics of the nineteenth century. Donald Ringe recognized years ago that, in a very important sense, *The Awakening* "is a powerful romantic novel."[12] Chopin's descriptive passages about sea and land are symbolically equivalent to Herman Melville's last paragraphs from "The Lee Shore" in *Moby-Dick* (1851).

> Know ye, now, Bulkington? Glimpses do ye see of that mortally intolerable truth; that all deep, earnest thinking is but the intrepid effort of the soul to keep the open independence of her sea; while the wildest winds of heaven and earth conspire to cast her on the treacherous, slavish shore?
>
> But as in landlessness alone resides the highest truth, shoreless, indefinite as God—so, better is it to perish in that howling infinite, than be ingloriously dashed upon the lee, even if that were safety! For worm-like, then, oh! who would craven crawl to land! Terrors of the terrible; is all this agony so vain? Take heart, take heart, O Bulkington! Bear thee grimly, demigod! Up from the spray of thy ocean-perishing—straight up, leaps thy apotheosis![13]

Even some of Chopin's metaphors for the sea are remarkably like Melville's: "For worm-like, then, oh! who would craven crawl to land!" ("like worms struggling blindly toward inevitable annihilation" [58]); "Up from the spray of thy ocean-perishing" ("Venus rising from the foam" [111]); "demigod" and "apotheosis" (the Gulf Spirit choosing Edna as one of the "semi-celestials" [30]). Ottavio Mark Casale observes that this passage also houses the deep irony that "while the sea-striver faces spiritual death on land, and while he knows that 'in landlessness alone resides the highest truth, shoreless, indefinite as God,' that way lies also actual death."[14] This, of course, will be Edna's fate as well.

Edna finds the shore hard to resist. Land values—safety, society, support—are seductive, and being alone, understandably, causes "ungovernable dread." True independence forces a keener sense of life's risks; the illusion of dependence sometimes can falsely quiet the anxieties of a day, or of a life. Choosing a solitary life forces the issue of death to surface because admitting that we are alone is philosophically very close to admitting that we will die.

It is therefore not surprising that Edna, beginning in chapter 10 to sense how alone she is, sees death in the deep waters of the Gulf. "A quick vision of death smote her soul, and for a second of time appalled and enfeebled her senses" (29). It is interesting, too, that her first swim, as well as many other significant moments throughout the novel, occurs at night, a very central image in Chopin. Edna's "night" often resembles the "dark night" Charles Peake describes: it "[stirs] intimations of mortality and a consciousness of melancholy isolation . . . and it [provokes] thoughts of the inconceivable vastness of the universe and the insignificance of mankind's place in it."[15] Edna cannot talk about her close proximity to death in the sea after she regains the safety of the shore. Chopin writes, "She made no mention of her encounter with death and her flash of terror, except to say to her husband, 'I thought I should have perished out there alone'" (29). It is significant that when Robert claims to understand how she feels after her terrifying swim, Edna rebuffs him: "You don't know anything about it. Why should you know?" (29). Though sensitive to Edna, Robert—conventional, social, and shore-minded—will probably never understand the painful lessons of the lonely sea.

By remembering the details of Edna's first long swim in chapter 10 as we examine chapter 39, we better understand and appreciate her growth. The sea has become a kind of transcendental symbol to Edna, and she approaches it with a sense of all it has come to mean. It is the enormous possibility of the self, "gleaming with the million lights of the sun" (113), and the only place she has ever been able to be completely alone. In chapter 10 others were not far behind, but now she will enter the sea without anyone standing along the shore to hear her should she call. The image of extreme solitude is enhanced further by the description of the desolate and broad beach: "All along the white beach, up and down, there was no living thing in sight" (113).

A gesture of self-celebration occurs at the water's edge in chapter 39. Edna removes her bathing suit and stands naked in the breeze. "How strange and awful it seemed to stand naked under the sky! how delicious! She felt like some new-born creature, opening its eyes in a familiar world that it had never known" (113). Edna is no longer the "tottering, stumbling, clutching child" (28) of chapter 10, just beginning to realize her powers. She is boldly, actively involved in the symbolism of her last swim, shedding the one garment that might still link her to the shore.

We recall Botticelli's *Birth of Venus* when we read this description. We also are reminded of the original myth of Aphrodite's birth and Chopin's important alterations of it. Unlike the classical version in which the violent Cronus is responsible for Aphrodite's birth, here Aphrodite gives birth to herself. There is violence in both episodes, of course. But in the myth Aphrodite is born from the violence of separation and dismemberment. Cronus cuts off his father's genitals and throws them into the sea; Aphrodite rises from the foam that gathers around them. But Edna's suicide occurs from the violence of union. She chooses to become one with the salty sea, the very place where life originates.

This union hints at the possibility of positive and important connection with the physical environment, with that part of the world, we remember from Gilman, that women had been cut off from through the century's prescriptive definitions of domestic space. Edna begins to realize the abundant wonder and joy of the universe and the natural world, and her connection to it all. Symbolically, the sea begins Edna's union with all other creatures, for water is common to all life. Edna seems to be moving toward a more expansive concept of human experience. Cristina Giorcelli proposes that "through her final sensuous and mystic ecstasy, seeking immersion in her environment, she either purges herself of her narrowly conceived individualism or exorcises the isolation into which she was cast" (139). Marilynne Robinson also finds Edna's immersion in the universe extremely hopeful. "The novel is not a simulated case study," she writes, "but an exploration of the solitary soul still enchanted by the primal, charged, and intimate encounter of naked sensation with the astonishing world" (xx).

Certainly it is hinted that the discovery of our vital connections to the self and to our world might lead to the discovery of our vital connections to others. Mary Papke writes, "Yet one also sees in Edna's life . . . intimations of alternatives to alienation and self-annihilation, a new 'structure of feeling,' as Raymond Williams called it, an embryonic social consciousness which cannot yet be fully articulated either by character or creator."[16] For the most part, however, the discovery of a meaningful "social consciousness" will be the task for women after Edna Pontellier.

Edna's first swim in chapter 10 is reckless initially; she does not realize the danger she is in until she is far out in the water. She thinks, "How easy it is!" Aloud, she says, "It is nothing, . . . why did I not discover before that it was nothing. Think of the time I have lost splashing about like a baby!" (28). The horror sets in only after she looks toward the shore and realizes she may not have the strength to return. Although Edna does not escape fear entirely in her second swim, she is truly a bolder swimmer, and a bolder woman, than she had been during the summer months on Grand Isle. From the moment her foot enters the water there are dangers, but Edna does not turn back. It has taken great courage to come this far. "She walked out. The water was chill, but she walked on. The water was deep, but she lifted her white body and reached out with a long, sweeping stroke" (113). Chopin's syntax, marked by the repetition of the conjunction *but*, emphasizes Edna's new determination to counter her fear.

During this swim Edna does not choose to look back to the shore and its security. She remembers the terror of her first swim but determines not to give in to it. "She remembered the night she swam far out, and recalled the terror that seized her at the fear of being unable to regain the shore. She did not look back now, but went on and on, thinking of the blue-grass meadow that she had traversed when a little child, believing that it had no beginning and no end" (113–14). Edna will never again return to shore.

In the last paragraph of the novel, "the old terror flamed up for an instant" (114). The "old terror," we are led to believe, refers to Edna's vision of death during her moonlight swim of chapter 10. But in the book's final scene the terror is even briefer, and "then [it] sank again" (114). The terror also seems slightly different. In chapter 10 fear wells up in Edna while she is considering the terrible distance to the shore; in chapter 39 fear seizes her while she is looking "into the distance" of the ocean. The first scene of terror is about the fear of death; the second, about the fear of possibility.

The book, as Chopin so significantly tells us in her early description of Edna's awakening, is about "the beginning of things" (15). The beginning of selfhood. The beginning of a new century. Only by giving birth to the self can a new self—and a more modern literature based on self-consciousness—ever be born. It is no small coincidence that a novel about the birth of the self ends with a woman returning to the sea, the source of life, of beginnings, nor that this return is coupled with images of childhood and early memories, emphasizing her return to the important beginnings of self-understanding. It seems almost uncanny that in 1893 Sigmund Freud and Joseph Breuer published the document that heralded the arrival of psychoanalysis, *The Psychic Mechanism of Hysterical Phenomena*. And in 1899 Freud published *The Interpretation of Dreams*. At the very moment Chopin was inviting psychoanalysis of Edna, the theory was being created.

That the sea at the novel's end is extremely maternal has been noted by critics such as Sandra Gilbert and Harold Bloom. Bloom calls it a "mothering sea" and writes, "Whitman's 'dark mother always gliding near with soft feet' has come to deliver Edna from the burden of being a mother, and indeed from all burden of otherness, forever."[17] Some critics, such as Cyrille Arnavon, Ruth Smith, Stewart Sullivan, and Elizabeth Fox-Genovese, have seen Edna's return to the womb of the sea as evidence of regression. But the ambiguous sea supports the puzzling but wonderful possibility that we are to view Edna not as dead but, rather, as yet unborn.

In fact, if we are to believe Emerson's assertion in "Self-Reliance" that "imitation is suicide" (1841, 259), we might find still another argument for a more hopeful view of things: since Edna, by walking into the sea, refuses imitation, her gesture must be seen within the romantic tradition as something other than suicide. Or perhaps we are to see the metaphor as foreshadowing important feminist messages about women recovering their mothers' memories and about giving birth to themselves, without the help of Cronuses or other men. Certainly Chopin's image anticipates the prominence and complexity of the birth metaphor in literature by women throughout the twentieth century.

There is no question that Edna Pontellier falls short of being and doing all that she might have. Judith Fryer is too generous in her assessment of Edna when she writes, "The suicide scene of *The Awakening* is the fulfillment of Edna's awakening."[18] In many ways she truly is unborn, unawakened. We could even argue that she is still, to some extent, a version of the parrot that announces Chopin's text. She has escaped from her cage and chosen to stop imitating those around her, but she has been unable to discover what she will do instead. She does not buy brushes and canvas and head for Paris. As Virginia Kouidis notes, Edna the artist does not fully exploit the Emersonian legacy to creativity implicit in the novel's pages, the legacy of "colored subjective vision" and "unresolved perception," the legacy that Kouidis claims early female modernists like Dorothy Richardson, Mina Loy, and Marianne Moore did find the courage to embrace.[19]

Edna does not contact Carrie Chapman and join the National American Woman Suffrage Association. She shows no interest in trying to form a truly egalitarian relationship with a man who could be her equal, a man such as the journalist Gouvernail.[20] She does not turn to friends capable of offering true sympathy, understanding, support, and wisdom. The image of the bird reeling toward the water is certainly a symbol of her partial failure: the caged bird escapes but can fly for only a brief time. Lawrence Thornton compares Edna to Icarus and believes she flies too close to the sun; the bird falling from the air, he argues, "becomes her memento mori" (1988, 142).

But to judge Edna, as Allen Stein so rightly notes, is clearly not what Chopin had in mind. The ambiguity she introduces, through her neutral narrator and complex image patterns, Stein argues, shows "that Chopin means to drive home upon her readers the realization that examination of complex human behavior involves one inevitably in so many tangled strands as to make moral judgment impossible." Stein's words remind us of Chopin's description of "the beginning of things": "necessarily vague, tangled, chaotic, and exceedingly disturbing" (15). Stein continues, "Difficult to attain, certainly, but not beyond human reach, though, are understanding and sympathy, and it is these, Chopin implies, toward which one should strive in looking at the case of Edna Pontellier."[21]

Chopin's novel, like much of her best short fiction throughout the 1890s, is about beginnings, not endings and resolutions. Eleanor Wymard writes, "The end of the novel is a revelation of human possibilities, not a nihilistic cure for feminine oppression."[22] Margaret Mitsutani expresses this another way: "It might be argued that Edna's awakening is, more than anything, a realization of what she is not."[23] And John Carlos Rowe believes *The Awakening* "is potentially a narrative of emancipation."[24]

The Awakening is a metaphor of possibility and potential rather than a didactic guidebook for the twentieth century, or for its writers. It is, as Joseph Urgo calls it, "a prologue to rebellion."[25] Like her name ("Pontellier," as Wendy Martin observes, means "one who bridges" [25]), Edna herself is one whose mission is to begin the painful process of bridging two centuries, two worlds, two visions of gender. So appropriate as a turn-of-the-century piece, *The Awakening* is about the beginning of selfhood, not its completion.

Angeline Goreau, the biographer of Aphra Behn, discusses the contradictions and disappointments in Aphra's life, many of which we also sense in the life of Edna—and in the life of Chopin herself. "One Aphra," she writes, "could not live without independence, the other could not give up her dependence." But Goreau understands Aphra's dilemma in much the same way as I think we are meant to understand Edna's. "Aphra's dilemma proceeded precisely from her radical attempt to be free; for new roles do not replace old ones in a single moment of realization, or even over centuries. The struggle for freedom is not linear but dialectic; the price of change is doubleness, and out of the contradiction emerges a new self."[26]

Can we really say that we would be happier with Chopin's novel if Edna had figured everything out? If she had not mysteriously walked into the Gulf? Would the book really have been a better one, as many critics have suggested, had Edna found an answer to the enormous questions she is presented with? Is that what Chopin intended, but failed, to accomplish?

It is important to remember that the last regret Edna has before leaving us forever is that she probably will never be understood. Thinking of Robert, she begins, "He did not know; he did not understand. He would never understand. Perhaps Doctor Mandelet would have understood if she had seen him—" (114). Emerson finds an important common denominator in all great people, and we might expand his observation to include all great characters in fiction. "Is it so bad, then," he asks, "to be misunderstood? Pythagoras was misunderstood, and Socrates, and Jesus, and Luther, and Copernicus, and Galileo, and Newton, and every pure and wise spirit that ever took flesh. To be great is to be misunderstood" (1841, 265). The misunderstanding that surrounds Edna's personal history, as well as the history of Chopin's novel itself, attests to the greatness of both Edna and her creator.

As indicated by the numerous new editions that appear yearly, *The Awakening* continues to attract readers. Its universality and twentieth-century appeal come precisely from Chopin's decision *not* to complete Edna's journey toward selfhood. She chooses only to define its pain and promise. Many of us who come to the book have found ourselves where Edna is, precisely on the brink of a personal beginning. Because her story ends prematurely, ends exactly as it does, we are forced to think hard about her life, and about our own. Because Edna fails to find answers, we search for them for her—and in the process, we find ourselves.

Notes

1. Background to the Novel

1. J. W. Buel, ed., *Louisiana and the Fair: An Exposition of the World, Its People, and Their Achievements*, vol. 10 (St. Louis: World's Progress Publishing Co., 1905), 3846.

2. *St. Louis and the World's Fair: An Illustrated Courier and Advance Souvenir of the Louisiana Purchase Exposition* (St. Louis: Robert Allan Reid, 1904), 3–4; hereafter cited in the text as *Advance Souvenir*.

3. *Official Guide to the Louisiana Purchase Exposition* (St. Louis: Louisiana Purchase Exposition Co., 1904), 46–51.

4. John Wesley Hanson, *The Official History of the Fair, St. Louis, 1904: The Sights and Scenes of the Louisiana Purchase Exposition* ([n.p.], 1904), 22; hereafter cited in the text.

5. Henry Adams, *The Education of Henry Adams*, in *Henry Adams: Novels, "Mont St. Michel," "The Education"*, ed. Ernest Samuels and Jayne N. Samuels (1907; New York: Library of America, 1983), 1146–47.

6. William Schuyler, "Kate Chopin," *The Writer* 7 (August 1894): 116.

7. Per Seyersted, *Kate Chopin: A Critical Biography* (Baton Rouge: Louisiana State University Press, 1969), 84; hereafter cited in the text.

8. Mary P. Ryan, *Womanhood in America: From Colonial Times to the Present* (New York: New Viewpoints, 1975), 196; hereafter cited in the text.

9. Mrs. George Black, F. R. G. S., as told to Elizabeth Bailey Price, *My Seventy Years* (London: Thomas Nelson and Sons, Ltd., 1938), 93.

10. Clarice Stasz, *American Dreamers: Charmian and Jack London* (New York: St. Martin's Press, 1988), 69.

11. Kathleen Barry, *Susan B. Anthony: A Biography of a Singular Feminist* (New York: Ballantine, 1988), 310; hereafter cited in the text.

12. Susan B. Anthony, Inscription, in *Life of Susan B. Anthony*, by Ida Husted Harper, vol. 1 (Indianapolis and Kansas City: Bowen-Merrill, 1899). This book is owned by Susan B. Anthony's first cousin, four generations removed—Gayle Uhler of Hiram College.

13. Charles Anthony, *Genealogy of the Anthony Family from 1495 to 1904* (Sterling, Ill.: privately published, 1904), 220.

14. Charlotte Perkins Gilman, *Women and Economics*, ed. Carl N. Degler (Boston: Small, Maynard & Co., 1898; New York: Harper & Row, 1966), 220; hereafter cited in the text.

15. Larzer Ziff, *The American 1890s: Life and Times of a Lost Generation* (New York: Viking Press, 1966), 283; hereafter cited in the text.

16. Thomas P. Getz, "Since My Daughter Plays on the Typewriter," arranged by George W. Hetzel, in *The Land of Contrasts 1880–1901*, ed. Neil Harris (New York: George Braziller, 1970), 326–29.

17. Linda Kerber and Jane DeHart-Mathews, eds., *Women's America: Refocusing the Past*, 2d ed. (New York: Oxford University Press, 1987), 221–25.

18. Mary Kelley, *Private Woman, Public Stage: Literary Domesticity in Nineteenth-Century America* (New York: Oxford University Press, 1984), viii–ix; hereafter cited in the text.

19. Kate Chopin, *At Fault*, in *The Complete Works of Kate Chopin*, ed. Per Seyersted, vol. 2 (Baton Rouge: Louisiana State University Press, 1969), 873.

20. William Dean Howells, *A Modern Instance* (Boston: Houghton Mifflin and Company, 1881), 509.

21. William Dean Howells, *Criticism and Fiction* (1891; New York: Harper and Brothers, 1893), 10–12; hereafter cited in the text.

22. T. DeWitt Talmage, *Social Dynamite: or, The Wickedness of Modern Society* (St. Louis: Holloway & Co., 1888), 178, 181.

23. Sarah Stage, *Female Complaints: Lydia Pinkham and the Business of Women's Medicine* (New York: W. W. Norton & Co., 1979), 180.

24. Margaret Culley, "The Context of *The Awakening*," in *The Awakening: An Authoritative Text, Contexts, and Criticism*, ed. Margaret Culley (New York: W. W. Norton & Co., 1976), 118–19. Hereafter, translations from the French are Culley's.

25. Max Rheinstein, "The Code and the Family," in *The Code Napoleon and the Common-Law World*, ed. Bernard Schwartz (New York: New York University Press, 1956; Westport, Conn.: Greenwood Press, 1975), 147.

26. Marie Fletcher, "The Southern Woman in the Fiction of Kate Chopin," *Louisiana History* 7 (Spring 1966): 118.

Notes

27. *Board of Lady Managers of the Louisiana Purchase Exposition Authorized by Act of Congress March III MDCCCCI* (Cambridge: H. O. Houghton and Co./Riverside Press, 1905), 325.

28. Mary L. Shaffter, "Creole Women," *The Chautauquan Circle* 15 (June 1892): 347; reprinted in Culley, *Awakening*, 121.

2. The Importance of the Work

1. Frank Norris, *McTeague* (1899; New York: Signet, 1964), 28, 66.

2. Barbara Solomon, ed., introduction to *"The Awakening" and Selected Stories of Kate Chopin* (New York: Signet, 1976), xxv.

3. Kate Chopin, "As You Like It," in *Complete Works*, vol. 2, 714.

4. Bernard Koloski, preface to *Approaches to Teaching Chopin's "The Awakening"*, ed. Bernard Koloski (New York: Modern Language Association of America, 1988), ix.

3. Critical Reception

1. Kate Chopin, "Aims and Autographs of Authors," *Book News* 17 (July 1899): 612; reprinted in *A Kate Chopin Miscellany*, ed. Per Seyersted and Emily Toth (Natchitoches, La.: Northwestern State University Press, 1979), 137.

2. Frances Porcher, "Kate Chopin's Novel," *St. Louis Mirror*, 4 May 1899, 6; reprinted in Culley, *Awakening*, 145–46.

3. Emily Toth, *Kate Chopin: A Life of the Author of "The Awakening"* (New York: William Morrow and Co., 1990), 367–69, 422–25; hereafter cited in the text.

4. Chopin showed her concern only through her witty and cynical retraction and her somewhat anxious question to her publisher two months after the book's release: "What are the prospects for the book?" ("Letter to Herbert S. Stone," 7 June 1899, in Seyersted and Toth, *Chopin Miscellany*, 137).

5. Felix Chopin, "Statement on Kate Chopin," interview with Charles van Ravenswaay, 19 January 1949, in Seyersted and Toth, *Chopin Miscellany*, 167.

6. Daniel S. Rankin, *Kate Chopin and Her Creole Stories* (Philadelphia: University of Pennsylvania Press, 1932), 177, 175.

7. Arthur Hobson Quinn, *American Fiction: An Historical and Critical Survey* (New York: Appleton-Century, 1936), 354–57.

8. Carlos Baker, "Delineation of Life and Character," in *Literary History of the United States*, ed. Robert E. Spiller, et al., vol. 2 (New York: MacMillan Co., 1948), 858–59. This identical entry was used in Spiller's revised, one-volume edition prepared in 1953, as well as in his third edition of 1963.

9. Joseph J. Reilly, *Of Books and Men* (New York: Julian Messner, 1942), 136.

10. Cyrille Arnavon, ed. and trans., introduction to *Edna* by Kate Chopin (Paris: Club bibliophile de France, 1953), 14.

11. The interest in the comparison between *The Awakening* and *Madame Bovary* continues to the present. See Elaine Jasenas, "The French Influence in Kate Chopin's *The Awakening*," *Nineteenth-Century French Studies* 4 (Spring 1976): 312–22.

12. Van Wyck Brooks, *Makers and Finders: A History of the Writer in America 1800–1915*, vol. 5, *The Confident Years: 1885–1915* (New York: E. P. Dutton & Co., 1952), 341; hereafter cited in the text.

13. Kenneth Eble, "A Forgotten Novel: Kate Chopin's *The Awakening*," *Western Humanities Review* 10, no. 3 (Summer 1956): 263, 269; hereafter cited in the text.

14. George Arms, "Kate Chopin's *The Awakening* in the Perspective of Her Literary Career," in *Essays on American Literature in Honor of Jay B. Hubbell*, ed. Clarence Gohdes (Durham: Duke University Press, 1967), 215; hereafter cited in the text.

15. Lewis Leary, "Kate Chopin's Other Novel," *Southern Literary Journal* 1 (Autumn 1968): 60–74. Bernard J. Koloski discussed this novel in the 1970s in "The Structure of Kate Chopin's *At Fault*," *Studies in American Fiction* 3 (Spring 1975): 89–94. I focused on it in 1980 in "Bright-Hued Feathers and Japanese Jars: Objectification of Character in Kate Chopin's *At Fault*," *Revue de Louisiane—Louisiana Review* 9, no. 1 (Summer 1980): 27–35. At the Third Kate Chopin Conference at Northwestern State University of Louisiana in Natchitoches, Louisiana, April 1-3, 1993, new papers on *At Fault* were presented by Karen M. Poremski, Jane Hotchkiss, and Pamela Glenn Menke.

16. Joan Zlotnick, "A Woman's Will: Kate Chopin on Selfhood, Wifehood, and Motherhood," *Markham Review* 3 (October 1968): 1–5.

17. Stanley Kauffman, "The Really Lost Generation," *New Republic* 155 (3 December 1966), 22, 37–38.

18. Lewis Leary, "Kate Chopin, Liberationist?" *Southern Literary Journal* 3 (Fall 1970): 138–44.

19. Cynthia Griffin Wolff, "Thanatos and Eros: Kate Chopin's *The Awakening*," *American Quarterly* 25 (October 1973): 450; hereafter cited in the text.

20. Nancy Walker, "Feminist or Naturalist: The Social Context of Kate Chopin's *The Awakening*," *Southern Quarterly* 17, no. 2 (1979): 95–103.

21. James H. Justus, "The Unawakening of Edna Pontellier," *Southern Literary Journal* 10 (Spring 1978): 107–22.

Notes

22. Lawrence Thornton, "*The Awakening*: A Political Romance," *American Literature* 52, no. 1 (March 1980): 51.

23. Lawrence Thornton, "Edna as Icarus: A Mythic Issue," in Koloski, *Approaches to "Awakening"*, 141; hereafter cited in the text.

24. Michael Gilmore, "Revolt against Nature: The Problematic Modernism of *The Awakening*," in *New Essays on "The Awakening"*, ed. Wendy Martin (Cambridge: Cambridge University Press, 1988), 60; hereafter cited in the text.

25. Linda Huf, *A Portrait of the Artist as a Young Woman: The Writer as Heroine in American Literature* (New York: Ungar, 1983), 79; hereafter cited in the text.

26. Emily Toth, "Kate Chopin's *The Awakening* as Feminist Criticism," *Louisiana Studies* 15 (Fall 1976): 242.

27. Elaine Showalter, "Tradition and the Female Talent: *The Awakening* as a Solitary Book," in Martin, *New Essays*, 50–51; hereafter cited in the text.

28. Andrew Delbanco, "The Half-Life of Edna Pontellier," in Martin, ed. *New Essays*, 89–107; hereafter cited in the text. Katherine Kearns, "The Nullification of Edna Pontellier," *American Literature* 63, no. 1 (March 1991): 62–88.

29. Peggy Skaggs, *Kate Chopin*, Twayne's United States Authors Series, edited by David J. Nordloh (Boston: Twayne Publishers, 1985), 111.

30. Patricia Hopkins Lattin, "Childbirth and Motherhood in Kate Chopin's Fiction," *Regionalism and the Female Imagination* 4 (Spring 1978): 8, 12; hereafter cited in the text.

31. Sandra M. Gilbert, "The Second Coming of Aphrodite: Kate Chopin's Fantasy of Desire," *Kenyon Review*, n.s. 5 (Summer 1983): 62; hereafter cited in the text. This essay was reprinted in Harold Bloom, ed., *Kate Chopin*, Modern Critical Views Series (New York: Chelsea House Publishers, 1987), 89–113; in revised form as the introduction to the Penguin edition of *"The Awakening" and Selected Stories by Kate Chopin* (1984); and as an essay in Sandra M. Gilbert and Susan Gubar's *No Man's Land, Sexchanges*, vol. 2 (New Haven: Yale University Press, 1989), 83–119.

32. Barbara C. Ewell, *Kate Chopin* (New York: Ungar, 1986), 158; hereafter cited in the text.

33. Cristina Giorcelli, "Edna's Wisdom: A Transitional and Numinous Merging," in Martin, *New Essays*, 110; hereafter cited in the text.

34. Marilynne Robinson, introduction to *"The Awakening" and Selected Short Stories by Kate Chopin* (New York: Bantam, 1988), viii; hereafter cited in the text.

35. Susan J. Rosowski, "The Novel of Awakening," *Genre* 12, no. 3 (Fall

1979): 313–32; Priscilla Leder, "An American Dilemma: Cultural Conflict in Kate Chopin's *The Awakening*," *Southern Studies* 22, no. 1 (1983): 97–104.

36. Cathy N. Davidson, foreword to *Kate Chopin Reconsidered: Beyond the Bayou*, ed. Lynda S. Boren and Sara deSaussure Davis (Baton Rouge: Louisiana State University Press, 1992), ix.

4. "A Green and Yellow Parrot . . ."

1. Kate Chopin, "Confidences," in *Complete Works*, vol. 2, 701.

2. Wendy Martin, introduction to Martin, *New Essays*, 25; hereafter cited in the text.

3. Anne Finch, *Selected Poems of Anne Finch, Countess of Winchilsea*, ed. Katharine M. Rogers (New York: Ungar, 1979), 56; hereafter cited in the text.

4. Elizabeth Barrett Browning, *Aurora Leigh*, intro. Gardner B. Taplin (1857; Chicago: Academy Chicago, 1979), 10; hereafter cited in the text.

5. Mary Elizabeth Coleridge, "The White Women" (1900), in *Norton Anthology of Literature by Women*, ed. Sandra M. Gilbert and Susan Gubar (New York: W. W. Norton and Co., 1985), 1165–66.

6. Ellen Moers, *Literary Women* (New York: Doubleday & Co., 1976), 247.

7. Flaubert uses the parrot image in yet another way in "*Un coeur simple*": as a symbol of sublimation. As Peter James Petersen points out, Chopin's "The White Eagle" (1900) is "reminiscent of Flaubert's '*un coeur simple*,' in which a woman who is systematically deprived of human contact sublimates all her longings in her relationship to a parrot, which is stuffed after she dies" ("The Fiction of Kate Chopin," Ph.D. diss., The University of New Mexico, 1972, 263). I discuss additional aspects of the eagle's ambiguity in my article, entitled "A Note on Kate Chopin's 'The White Eagle,'" *Arizona Quarterly* 40, no. 2 (Summer 1984), 189–92.

8. Gregory L. Candela discusses elaborate parallels between Chopin's use of the mockingbird and Whitman's in "Walt Whitman and Kate Chopin: A Further Connection," *Walt Whitman Review* 24, no. 4 (December 1978): 163–65.

9. Patricia S. Yaeger, "'A Language Which Nobody Understood': Emancipatory Strategies in *The Awakening*," *Novel: A Forum on Fiction* 20, no. 3 (Spring 1987): 203.

10. Kate Chopin, "Impressions: 1894," in Seyersted and Toth, *Chopin Miscellany*, 91.

11. Kate Chopin, "Lilacs," in *Complete Works*, Vol. 1, 361–62.

12. Kate Chopin, "Boulôt and Boulotte," in *Complete Works*, vol. 1, 151–52.

Notes

13. Elizabeth Fox-Genovese, "The Experience, Culture, and Values of Southern Women," in Koloski, *Approaches to "Awakening"*, 37.

14. Kate Chopin, "Emancipation: A Life Fable," in *Complete Works*, vol. 1, 37–38.

5. Keeping up with the Procession

1. Henry B. Fuller, *With the Procession*, intro. Mark Harris (1895; Chicago: University of Chicago Press, 1965), 57–58.

2. Kate Chopin, "A Reflection," in *Complete Works*, vol. 2, 622.

3. Margaret Culley points out in a footnote to *The Awakening: An Authoritative Text, Contexts, and Criticism* that a hurricane destroyed much of Grand Isle in 1893, dating the story prior to that year (3).

4. Henrik Ibsen, *Hedda Gabler* [1890], in *Norton Anthology of World Masterpieces*, ed. Maynard Mack, et al., vol. 2, 5th ed. (New York: W. W. Norton & Co., 1985), 1294. For other connections between Chopin and Ibsen, see Dorothy H. Jacobs, "*The Awakening*: A Recognition of Confinement," in Boren and Davis, *Chopin Reconsidered*, 80–94; see also William P. Warnken, "Kate Chopin and Henrik Ibsen: A Study of *The Awakening* and *A Doll's House*," *Massachusetts Studies in English* 5 (Winter 1975): 43–49.

5. Henry James, *The Notebooks of Henry James*, ed. F. O. Matthiessen and Kenneth B. Murdock (New York: Oxford University Press, 1947), 129.

6. Priscilla Allen, "Old Critics and New: The Treatment of Chopin's *The Awakening*," in *The Authority of Experience: Essays in Feminist Criticism*, ed. Arlyn Diamond and Lee R. Edwards (Amherst: University of Massachusetts Press, 1977), 231–34; hereafter cited in the text.

7. The selfishness of Léonce and other Creoles often takes the form of racial arrogance. Latins like Mariequita are treated as inferiors. Robert finds them, as a race, "not very congenial" (97). Black characters are treated with neglect or disdain. A small black girl sits on the floor by Madame Lebrun's sewing machine and works the treadle. In a sentence of quiet irony, Chopin registers her disapproval of the scene: "The Creole woman does not take any chances which may be avoided of imperiling her health" (22). Victor, Madame Lebrun's son, treats black servants in his mother's homes with the ruthless arrogance and condescension of a plantation overseer. And Léonce considers those he employs for domestic services innately inferior; he arrogantly reminds Edna that "they need looking after, like any class of persons that you employ" (52). Helen Taylor somewhat misses the irony Chopin uses to attack racism: "I would argue that Chopin's racism is a central element in her writing, and cannot be ignored or simply excused. As with King and Stuart, her inability or refusal to confront it created critical problems and

125

severely limited her achievement." And specifically about *The Awakening* she writes: "Its unconsciously racist elements cannot be excused, but its feminist subtext manages to explore and explode the various meanings of femininity in the postbellum South" (*Gender, Race, and Region in the Writings of Grace King, Ruth McEnery Stuart, and Kate Chopin* [Baton Rouge: Louisiana State University Press, 1989], 156, 202; hereafter cited in the text).

8. In *Showplace of America* (Kent, Ohio: Kent State University Press, 1991), Jan Cigliano hints at a similar concern of the Cleveland wealthy between 1850 and 1910. Mansions were erected on major streets throughout America's big cities in the nineteenth century and then filled with opulent furnishings and art objects. Cigliano describes the palatial homes built along Cleveland's Euclid Avenue. She mentions that John D. Rockefeller's Euclid Avenue residence had a maid as its sole occupant for many years.

9. Frances Hartley, *The Ladies' Book of Etiquette* and *Manual of Politeness* (1875); reprinted in Culley, *Awakening*, 50.

10. Bert Bender, "The Teeth of Desire: *The Awakening* and *The Descent of Man*," *American Literature* 63, no. 3 (September 1991): 472.

11. Alice Walker, "Zora Neale Hurston: A Cautionary Tale and a Partisan View," in *In Search of Our Mothers' Gardens* (New York: Harcourt Brace Jovanovich, 1984), 90.

12. Anne Bradstreet, "The Prologue" to *The Tenth Muse* (1650), in Gilbert and Gubar, *Norton Anthology*, 62.

6. Goddesses and Mythic Scenes

1. William Secker, *A Wedding Ring, Fit for the Finger* (Boston, 1750); quoted in Ryan, *Womanhood in America*, 27.

2. Giorcelli also points out the significant detail that 28 August is the day Christians celebrate St. Augustine, a man who saw vast inequalities between both man and God, and man and woman.

3. Sir James George Frazer, *The Golden Bough* (1922; reprinted in a one-volume abridged edition, New York: Macmillan, 1963), 163; hereafter cited in the text.

4. John R. May, "Local Color in *The Awakening*," *Southern Review* 6 (Autumn 1970): 1033.

5. Culley writes about Esplanade Street in an annotation to *The Awakening*: "Called 'Promenade Publique' in the 1830s, it was a street of palatial homes shaded by live oaks, palms, and magnolias" (50).

6. Lafcadio Hearn, *Chita: A Memory of Last Island* (1889; New York: Harper & Brothers, 1917), 14–15.

7. For further comparisons between the island symbolism of Hearn and Chopin, see Joyce Dyer, "Lafcadio Hearn's *Chita* and Kate Chopin's *The*

Awakening: Two Naturalistic Tales of the Gulf Islands," *Southern Studies* 23, no. 4 (Winter 1984): 412–26.

8. Kate Chopin, "At Chênière Caminada," in *Complete Works*, vol. 1, 309–18.

9. This image, as well as others in *The Awakening*, invites interesting parallels between Chopin's "sea" stories and Jack London's fiction, most particularly *Martin Eden* (New York: Grosset & Dunlap, 1908). In *Martin Eden*, for example, Martin conquers a "mad desire" to "let go sheet and tiller and to clasp [Ruth] in his arms" (174). The moon is highly significant in this London novel, there is the same Edenic wordplay that we find in *The Awakening* (Edna, Martin Eden), and lines are quoted from Swinburne.

10. For a more elaborate treatment of Tonie's repression and "At Chênière Caminada," see Joyce Dyer, "Kate Chopin's Sleeping Bruties," *Markham Review* 9, no. 1 (Summer 1980): 27–35, reprinted in Bloom.

11. Much has been made of Oscar Chopin's drawing of his mother's parlor. It shows a naked Venus she apparently kept on a bookshelf.

12. Chopin frequently uses references to Texas, as well as Texan characters in her fiction as a kind of shorthand. For a more expansive discussion of this technique, see Joyce Dyer and Robert Emmett Monroe, "Texas and Texans in the Fiction of Kate Chopin," *Western American Literature* 20, no. 1 (May 1985), 3–15.

13. For a more detailed analysis of Gouvernail's roles in Chopin fiction, see Joyce Dyer, "Gouvernail, Kate Chopin's Sensitive Bachelor," *Southern Literary Journal* 14, no. 1 (Fall 1981): 46–55, reprinted in Bloom.

14. Kate Chopin, "Athénaïse," in *Complete Works*, vol. 1, 426–54.

15. Algernon Swinburne, "A Cameo," in *Poems and Ballads*, First Series (London: Edward Moxon and Co., 1866; London: William Heinemann Ltd., 1924), 113.

16. Margaret Culley, "Edna Pontellier: 'A Solitary Soul,'" in *Awakening*, 228; hereafter cited in the text.

17. Nina Baym, introduction to *"The Awakening" and Selected Stories by Kate Chopin* (New York: Modern Library, 1981), xxxviii.

18. Bernard Koloski, "Notes: The Swinburne Lines in *The Awakening*," *American Literature* 45 (1974): 609.

19. The fact that Swinburne's eroticism had masochistic roots might also suggest yet another warning to Edna: sex necessarily had a violent component born of the perhaps inevitable power division between subject and object. As we know from Morse Peckham, "Swinburne was an active masochist: he could achieve sexual pleasure only through suffering, specifically through being beaten" (introduction, in *Swinburne: Poems and Ballads* [1866]; *Atalanta in Calydon* [1865], ed. Morse Peckham (New York: Bobbs-Merrill, 1970).

7. "Couldst Thou But Know": Edna's Pursuit of the Beloved

1. Kate Chopin, "'Crumbling Idols' by Hamlin Garland," in *Complete Works*, vol. 2, 693–94.

2. Louisa May Alcott, *Little Women* (1860; New York: Grosset & Dunlap, 1947), 228; hereafter cited in the text.

3. Interestingly, Showalter notices that references to "Chopin" also function as what Nancy K. Miller calls the "internal female signature" (In a note, Showalter thanks Miller of Barnard College for this phrase. It will appear in a work-in-progress by Miller on women's writing in France). Showalter believes that Chopin's use of a composer who shares her name becomes "a literary punning signature that alludes to Kate Chopin's ambitions as an artist and to the emotions she wished her book to arouse in its readers" (1988, 47).

4. Lyle Saxon, *Lafitte the Pirate* (New York: Century Co., 1930), 290–98.

5. In Chopin's "Vagabonds," a brilliant story very neglected by scholars (written in 1895, but not published until 1932 by Rankin, and then only once more, in 1969 by Seyersted), slime and mud become the emblems of Valcour—the vagabond who represents the narrator's alter ego. I presented a rediscovery piece about "Vagabonds" at the Third Kate Chopin Conference, entitled "'Vagabonds': A Story Without a Home."

6. Cynthia Griffin Wolff interprets the absence of a kiss both after Edna awakens on the Chênière and after she returns from the birth scene as an indication that "Edna's libidinal energies have been arrested at a pre-genital level." For example, for Wolff, Edna's immediate concern with food upon her awakening (rather than sex) certifies the destructive oral fixation that will lead, in part, to her disintegration (461–62).

7. "'Is Love Divine?' The Question Answered by Three Ladies Well Known in St. Louis Society," *St. Louis Post-Dispatch*, 16 January 1898, 17; quoted in Toth, *Chopin*, 310, and in Emily Toth, "Kate Chopin on Divine Love and Suicide: Two Rediscovered Articles," *American Literature* 63, no. 1 (March 1991): 118.

8. "I Am Becoming an Artist. Think of It!"

1. James Huneker, *Overtones* (New York, 1904), 286; quoted in Judith Tick, "Passed Away Is the Piano Girl: Changes in American Musical Life, 1870–1900," in *Women Making Music*, ed. Jane Bowers and Judith Tick (Chicago: University of Illinois Press, 1987), 325.

2. Carol Neuls-Bates, ed., *Women in Music: An Anthology of Source Readings from the Middle Ages to the Present* (New York: Harper & Row, 1982), xiii.

Notes

3. Léonce's opinion about women and music is representative of much critical opinion of his time. The work of the brilliant American composer-pianist Amy Marcy Cheney Beach (composer of the first symphony by an American woman ever to be performed), though popular and successful, suffered from "much contemporary critical commentary [that] dwelt on the fact that Beach was a woman, hence her works could not be compared to those of mainstream male composers" (Adrienne Fried Block, assisted by Nancy Stewart, "Women in American Music, 1800–1918," in *Women and Music*, ed. Karin Pendle [Bloomington: Indiana University Press, 1991], 170).

4. Germaine Greer, *The Obstacle Race: The Fortunes of Women Painters and Their Work* (New York: Farrar, Straus & Giroux, 1979), 310; hereafter cited in the text.

5. Deborah E. Barker closely examines Edna's attempt to paint Adèle (including elaborate comments on "pictorial representations of the Madonna" [64]) in her study, entitled "The Awakening of Female Artistry," included in Boren and deSaussure, *Kate Chopin Reconsidered*, 61–79.

6. Kate Chopin, "Wiser Than a God," in *Complete Works*, vol. 1, 39–47; hereafter cited in the text as "Wiser."

7. There were, of course, a few exceptions. For a discussion of American female pianists who made public performances during the nineteenth and twentieth centuries, see Christine Ammer, "Seated at the Keyboard," in *Unsung: A History of Women in American Music* (Westport, Conn.: Greenwood Press, 1980), 43–70.

8. John B. Vickery, *The Literary Impact of the Golden Bough* (Princeton: Princeton University Press, 1973), 320.

9. See my discussion of the theme of madness in other Chopin stories ("Mrs. Mobry's Reason" [1893] and "La Belle Zoraïde" [1894]) in "Techniques of Distancing in the Fiction of Kate Chopin," *Southern Studies* 24, no. 1 (Spring 1985): 69–81.

10. Elizabeth Fox-Genovese, "Kate Chopin's *The Awakening*," *Southern Studies* 18 (Fall 1979): 288.

11. Willa Cather, "Books and Magazines," *Pittsburgh Leader*, 8 July 1899, 6; reprinted in Culley, *Awakening*, 154.

12. Patricia Lattin, "The Search for Self in Kate Chopin's Fiction: Simple Versus Complex Vision," *Southern Studies* 21, no. 2 (1982): 223.

9. Understanding Edna's Suicide

1. John Brisben Walker, "Woman's Progress since the World's Fair at Chicago," *Cosmopolitan* [*The World's Fair*] 37, no. 5 (September 1904), 520. This issue was one of the items on display in the National Museum of

American History in Washington, D.C., 12 February–26 August 1992, as part of a special World's Fair exhibition.

2. Cather, in her *Pittsburgh Leader* review, blames Edna for expecting too much from her passion for Robert, for being "fanciful and romantic to the last" (6). George Spangler ("Kate Chopin's *The Awakening*: A Partial Dissent," *Novel: A Forum on Fiction* 3 [Spring 1970]) believes that Edna, at the end, "is unable to endure Robert's tender note of rejection"; in his view, Chopin's work is no more than "an ordinary sentimental novel" (252). In Elaine Showalter's early remarks about *The Awakening* in *A Literature of Their Own* (Princeton: Princeton University Press, 1977), she assesses Edna's final act: "Chopin's Edna Pontellier thinks 'it is better to wake up after all, even to suffer, rather than to remain a dupe to illusions all one's life'; but when her lover abandons her she drowns herself" (131). Showalter sees Edna in the tradition of heroines like Eliot's Maggie Tulliver rather than Brontë's Jane Eyre. Mary Jane Lupton in her article "Women Writers and Death by Drowning" in *Amid Visions and Revisions: Poetry and Criticism on Literature and the Arts*, ed. Burney J. Hollis (Baltimore: Morgan State University Press, 1985) feels that it must be recognized that Edna's "self-destruction is partly a response to being rejected by Robert, whom she loves." Lupton writes, "Killing oneself over a man I would call the Dido syndrome" (97).

3. "New Publications," *New Orleans Times-Democrat*, 18 June 1899, 15; reprinted in Culley, *The Awakening*, 150.

4. The word *musk* is derived from the Sanskrit *muska*, meaning "testicle" or "scrotum." Musk sacs located under the skin of a male musk deer's abdomen, for example, are scrotum-shaped.

5. Margaret Fuller, "Life without and Life within" (1859); quoted in Showalter, "Tradition and the Female Talent," 53. Showalter located this Fuller quotation in a work by Bell G. Chevigny, *The Woman and the Myth* (Old Westbury, N.Y.: Feminist Press, 1976), 279.

6. Mary Jo Salter, "A Poem of One's Own," *New Republic* 204 (4 March 1991): 34.

7. Herbert Ross Brown, *The Sentimental Novel in America, 1789–1860* (Durham: Duke University Press, 1940), 159.

8. A. S. Byatt, *Possession* (New York: Random House, 1990), 152.

9. Ralph Waldo Emerson, "Self-Reliance" [1841] in *Ralph Waldo Emerson: Essays and Lectures* (New York: Library of America, 1983), 263; hereafter cited in the text.

10. Ralph Waldo Emerson, "The Transcendentalist," lecture read at the Masonic Temple, Boston, January 1842; reprinted in *Ralph Waldo Emerson: Essays and Lectures* (New York: Library of America), 199–200.

11. Dorothy Goldman, "Kate Chopin's *The Awakening*: 'Casting Aside that Fictitious Self,'" in *The Modern American Novella*, ed. A. Robert Lee (New York: St. Martin's, 1989), 57.

Notes

12. Donald A. Ringe, "Romantic Imagery in Kate Chopin's *The Awakening*," *American Literature* 43 (January 1972): 587.

13. Herman Melville, *Moby-Dick*, in *Herman Melville: "Redburn," "White-Jacket," "Moby-Dick"* (1851; New York: Library of America, 1983), 906–7.

14. Ottavio Mark Casale, "Beyond Sex: The Dark Romanticism of Kate Chopin's *The Awakening*," *Ball State University Forum* 19, no. 1 (Winter 1978): 79.

15. Charles Peake, *Introduction to Poetry of the Landscape and the Night* (London: Edward Arnold, 1967), 9. For a more extensive examination of night imagery in Chopin, see Joyce Dyer, "Night Images in the Work of Kate Chopin," *American Literary Realism, 1870–1910* 14, no. 2 (Autumn 1981): 216–30.

16. Mary E. Papke, *Verging on the Abyss: The Social Fiction of Kate Chopin and Edith Wharton* (Westport, Conn.: Greenwood Press, 1990), 87.

17. Harold Bloom, introduction to Bloom, *Chopin*, 6.

18. Judith Fryer, "Edna Pontellier: The New Woman as Woman," in *The Faces of Eve: Women in the Nineteenth Century American Novel* (New York: Oxford University Press, 1976), 244.

19. Virginia M. Kouidis, "Prison into Prism: Emerson's 'Many-Colored Lenses' and the Woman Writer of Early Modernism," in *The Green American Tradition: Essays and Poems for Sherman Paul*, ed. H. Daniel Peck (Baton Rouge: Louisiana State University Press, 1989), 120–22.

20. For a more extensive study of a possible relationship between Edna and Gouvernail, see Joyce Dyer, "Gouvernail, Kate Chopin's Sensitive Bachelor."

21. Allen F. Stein, "Kate Chopin's *The Awakening* and the Limits of Moral Judgment," in *A Fair Day in the Affections: Literary Essays in Honor of Robert B. White, Jr.*, ed. Jack D. Durant and M. Thomas Hester (Raleigh, N.C.: Winston Press, 1980), 160.

22. Eleanor B. Wymard, "Kate Chopin: Her Existential Imagination," *Southern Studies* 19, no. 4 (Winter 1980): 384.

23. Margaret Mitsutani, "Kate Chopin's *The Awakening*: The Narcissism of Edna Pontellier," *Studies in English Literature* (1986): 14–15.

24. John Carlos Rowe, "The Economics of the Body in Kate Chopin's *The Awakening*," in Boren and Davis, *Chopin Reconsidered*, 140.

25. Joseph R. Urgo, "A Prologue to Rebellion: *The Awakening* and the Habit of Self-Expression," *Southern Literary Journal* 20, no. 1 (Fall 1987): 22.

26. Angeline Goreau, *Reconstructing Aphra: A Social Biography of Aphra Behn* (New York: Dial Press, 1980), 5.

Selected Bibliography

Primary Sources

At Fault. St Louis: Nixon-Jones Printing Co., 1890.

The Awakening. Chicago: Herbert S. Stone & Co., 1899.

The Awakening: An Authoritative Text, Contexts, Criticism. Edited by Margaret Culley. New York: W. W. Norton and Co., 1976.

Bayou Folk. Boston: Houghton Mifflin & Co., 1894.

The Complete Works of Kate Chopin. Edited by Per Seyersted. 2 vols. Baton Rouge: Louisiana State University Press, 1969.

A Kate Chopin Miscellany. Edited by Per Seyersted and Emily Toth. Natchitoches, La.: Northwestern State University Press, 1979.

A Night in Acadie. Chicago: Way & Williams, 1897.

A Vocation and a Voice. Edited and with an introduction and notes by Emily Toth. New York: Penguin Books, 1991.

Secondary Sources

Books and Parts of Books

Allen, Priscilla. "Old Critics and New: The Treatment of Chopin's *The Awakening*." In *The Authority of Experience: Essays in Feminist*

Criticism, edited by Arlyn Diamond and Lee R. Edwards, 224–38. Amherst: University of Massachusetts Press, 1977. Attacks new Chopin critics for judging Edna nearly as severely as old critics did.

Arnavon, Cyrille, ed. and trans. Introduction to *Edna* by Kate Chopin, 1–22. Paris: Club bibliophile de France, 1952. Calls *The Awakening* an American *Madame Bovary* but claims Edna's suicide is unjustified and regressive.

Bauer, Dale M. "Kate Chopin's *The Awakening*: Having and Hating Tradition." In *Feminist Dialogics: A Theory of Failed Community*, 129–58. Albany: State University of New York Press, 1988. Describes Edna's attempt to engage in subversive dialogue with Creole culture.

Baym, Nina. Introduction to *"The Awakening" and Selected Stories* by Kate Chopin, vii–xi. New York: Modern Library, 1981. Discusses the tradition of local color and how local color complements and enhances *The Awakening* and selected fiction.

Bloom, Harold, ed. *Kate Chopin*. Modern Critical Views Series. New York: Chelsea House Publishers, 1987. Contains an introduction by Bloom and reprints of essays by Kenneth Eble, Larzer Ziff, Donald A. Ringe, Cynthia Griffin Wolff, Susan J. Rosowski, Joyce C. Dyer, Elaine Gardiner, Sandra M. Gilbert, and Kathleen Margaret Lant.

Bonner, Thomas, Jr. *The Kate Chopin Companion, with Chopin's Translations from French Fiction*. Westport, Conn.: Greenwood Press, 1988. Contains French translations, a dictionary of important Chopin names and terms, period maps, and a bibliographic essay.

Boren, Lynda S., and Sara deSaussure Davis, eds. *Kate Chopin Reconsidered: Beyond the Bayou*. Baton Rouge: Louisiana State University Press, 1992. Fourteen essays by both established and new Chopin scholars represent a range of approaches to Chopin, including biographical, poststructuralist, and New Historicist.

Elfenbein, Anna Shannon. "Kate Chopin: From Stereotype to Sexual Realism." In *Women on the Color Line: Evolving Stereotypes and the Writings of George Washington Cable, Grace King, Kate Chopin*, 117–57. Charlottesville: University Press of Virginia, 1989. Concentrates on Edna's defiance of social conventions.

Ewell, Barbara C. *Kate Chopin*. New York: Ungar, 1986. Studies the development of Chopin's work, relating her growth to her private artistic decisions and reactions to public response.

Fryer, Judith. "Edna Pontellier: The New Woman as Woman." In *The Faces of Eve: Women in the Nineteenth Century American Novel*, 243–58. New York: Oxford University Press, 1976. Praises Edna as the culmination of the new woman in nineteenth-century fiction.

Selected Bibliography

Goldman, Dorothy. "Kate Chopin's *The Awakening*: 'Casting Aside that Fictitious Self.'" In *The Modern American Novella*, edited by A. Robert Lee, 48–65. New York: St. Martin's, 1989. Discusses techniques for the revelation of Edna's progress toward self-understanding.

Hirsch, Marianne. "Spiritual *Bildung*: The Beautiful Soul as Paradigm." In *The Voyage In: Fictions of Female Development*, edited by Elizabeth Abel, Marianne Hirsch, and Elizabeth Langland, 23–48. Hanover, N.H.: University Press of New England for Dartmouth College, 1983. Examines the female counterpart of the bildungsroman in novels by Johann Wolfgang von Goethe, George Eliot, Theodor Fontane, and Kate Chopin.

Hoder-Salmon, Marilyn. *Kate Chopin's "The Awakening": Screenplay as Interpretation*. Gainesville, Fla.: University Press of Florida, 1992. Adapts *The Awakening* into a screenplay for the purpose of scholarly interpretation.

Huf, Linda. "*The Awakening* (1899): Kate Chopin's Crimes against Polite Society." In *A Portrait of the Artist as a Young Woman: The Writer as Heroine in American Literature*, 58–79. New York: Ungar, 1983. Focuses on the contradictory messages of the society that locks Edna into the role of wife and mother.

Jones, Anne Goodwyn. "The Life behind the Mask." In *Tomorrow Is Another Day: The Woman Writer in the South, 1859–1936*, 135–82. Baton Rouge: Louisiana State University Press, 1981. Discusses Chopin's personal and fictional attempts to affirm individual vision.

Kate Chopin International Conference. *Perspectives on Kate Chopin: Proceedings of the Kate Chopin International Conference*. Natchitoches, La.: Northwestern State University Press, 1990. Includes reprints of twelve papers from the April 1989 conference, including an essay by Margit Stange that now appears in revised form in the 1993 Bedford Books edition of *The Awakening*.

Koloski, Bernard. ed. *Approaches to Teaching Chopin's "The Awakening"*. New York: Modern Language Association of America, 1988. Contains a diverse collection of critical and pedagogical essays about Chopin's novel; many are revised versions of previously published criticism.

Kouidis, Virginia M. "Prison into Prism: Emerson's 'Many- Colored Lenses' and the Woman Writer of Early Modernism." In *The Green American Tradition: Essays and Poems for Sherman Paul*, edited by H. Daniel Peck, 115–34. Baton Rouge: Louisiana State University Press, 1989. Looks at *The Awakening* as a point of departure for early female modernists like Dorothy Richardson, Mina Loy, and Marianne Moore.

Leary, Lewis. Introduction to *"The Awakening" and Other Stories* by Kate Chopin, iii–xviii. New York: Holt, Rinehart and Winston, 1970. Includes biographical background and identifies recurring patterns in fiction.

———. *Southern Excursions: Essays on Mark Twain and Others*. Baton Rouge: Louisiana State University Press, 1971. Contains reprints of two Leary essays on Chopin.

Martin, Wendy, ed. *New Essays on "The Awakening"*. Cambridge: Cambridge University Press, 1988. Contains an introduction by Martin and essays by Elaine Showalter, Michael Gilmore, Andrew Delbanco, and Cristina Giorcelli that question established assumptions and interpretations through new critical methods.

Papke, Mary. *Verging on the Abyss: The Social Fiction of Kate Chopin and Edith Wharton*. Westport, Conn.: Greenwood Press, 1990. Argues that both Chopin and Wharton offer feminist social critique through alienated characters.

Rankin, Daniel S. *Kate Chopin and Her Creole Stories*. Philadelphia: University of Pennsylvania Press, 1932. Biography that registers a preference for the Creole stories over *The Awakening* and includes interviews with Chopin's friends and family and 11 short stories.

Robinson, Marilynne. Introduction to *"The Awakening" and Selected Short Stories by Kate Chopin*, vii–xx. New York: Bantam, 1988. Praises the book's ambiguity.

St. Andrews, Bonnie. "Aphrodite Unencumbered: Kate Chopin's *The Awakening*." In *Forbidden Fruit: On the Relationship between Women and Knowledge in Doris Lessing, Selma Lagerlöf, Kate Chopin, Margaret Atwood*, 28–57. Troy, N.Y.: Whitston Publishing Co., 1986. Discusses Edna's quest for knowledge of good and evil.

Seyersted, Per. *Kate Chopin: A Critical Biography*. Baton Rouge: Louisiana State University Press, 1969. Literary biography, with emphasis on Chopin's movement toward increasing boldness in theme and artistry.

Skaggs, Peggy. *Kate Chopin*. Twayne's United States Authors Series, ed. David J. Nordloh. Boston: Twayne Publishers, 1985. Traces Chopin's theme of the search for identity throughout her fiction.

Solomon, Barbara, ed. Introduction to *"The Awakening" and Selected Short Stories of Kate Chopin*, vii–xvii. New York: Signet, 1976. Provides discussion of Chopin's short fiction as well as the revolutionary nature of *The Awakening*.

Stein, Allen F. "Kate Chopin." In *After the Vows Were Spoken: Marriage in American Literary Realism*, 163–208. Columbus: Ohio State University Press, 1984. Examines the drive for personal freedom in Chopin's marriage stories.

Selected Bibliography

————. "Kate Chopin's *The Awakening* and the Limits of Moral Judgment." In *A Fair Day in the Affections: Literary Essays in Honor of Robert B. White, Jr.*, edited by Jack D. Durant and M. Thomas Hester, 159–69. Raleigh, N.C.: Winston Press, 1980. Argues that ambiguity in *The Awakening* makes moral judgment impossible.

Taylor, Helen. "Kate Chopin." In *Gender, Race, and Region in the Writings of Grace King, Ruth McEnery Stuart, and Kate Chopin*, 138–202. Baton Rouge: Louisiana State University Press, 1989. Examines the important feminist subtext to be found in *The Awakening*, in spite of its unconscious racism.

Toth, Emily. *Kate Chopin: A Life of the Author of "The Awakening"*. New York: William Morrow and Co., 1990. A detailed feminist biography that documents numerous parallels between Chopin's life and work.

Treichler, Paula A. "The Construction of Ambiguity in *The Awakening*: A Linguistic Analysis." In *Women and Language in Literature and Society*, edited by Sally McConnell-Ginet, Ruth Borker, and Nelly Furman, 239–57. New York: Praeger, 1980. Illustrates how the grammar of *The Awakening* contributes to the book's ambiguity.

Walker, Nancy A., ed. *"The Awakening."* Boston: Bedford Books of St. Martin's Press, 1993. Provides not only an authoritative text, critical history, and background information, but also essays that discuss new critical theory and use new perspectives to analyze Chopin.

Ziff, Larzer. "The Abyss of Inequality: Sarah Orne Jewett, Mary Wilkins Freeman, Kate Chopin." In *The American 1890s: Life and Times of a Lost Generation*, 275–305. New York: Viking Press, 1966. Discusses the theme of female sexuality in Chopin's fiction.

Articles

Arner, Robert. "Kate Chopin," *Louisiana Studies* 14 (Spring 1975): 11–139. Book-length study that focuses on Chopin's psychological symbolism.

Bender, Bert. "The Teeth of Desire: *The Awakening* and *The Descent of Man*." *American Literature* 63, no. 3 (September 1991): 459–73. Studies Chopin's response to Darwin's *The Descent of Man and Selection in Relation to Sex* (1871).

Bonner, Thomas, Jr. "Kate Chopin's *At Fault* and *The Awakening*: A Study in Structure." *Markham Review* 7 (Fall 1977): 10–14. Examines the structural relationship between *At Fault* and *The Awakening*.

Candela, Gregory L. "Walt Whitman and Kate Chopin: A Further Connection." *Walt Whitman Review* 24, no. 4 (December 1978): 163–65. Compares Whitman's and Chopin's use of mockingbird imagery.

Cantwell, Robert. "*The Awakening* by Kate Chopin." *Georgia Review* 10 (Winter 1956): 489–94. Reviews Chopin's biography and praises her unique gift for depicting sensuous experience.

Casale, Ottavio Mark. "Beyond Sex: The Dark Romanticism of Kate Chopin's *The Awakening.*" *Ball State University Forum* 19, no. 1 (Winter 1978): 76–80. Compares Hawthorne and Melville with Chopin in terms of their use of romantic themes and imagery.

Cather, Willa. "Books and Magazines." *Pittsburgh Leader*, 8 July 1899, 6. Argues that, although exquisitely written, *The Awakening* suffers from the presentation of an overly sentimental and romantic heroine.

Dyer, Joyce. "Gouvernail, Kate Chopin's Sensitive Bachelor." *Southern Literary Journal* 14, no. 1 (Fall 1981): 46–55. Discusses the character of Gouvernail throughout Chopin's canon.

———. "Lafcadio Hearn's *Chita* and Kate Chopin's *The Awakening*: Two Naturalistic Tales of the Gulf Islands." *Southern Studies* 23, no. 4 (Winter 1984): 412–26. Compares Hearn's and Chopin's brands of naturalism.

———. "Night Images in the Work of Kate Chopin." *American Literary Realism, 1870–1910* 14, no. 2 (Autumn 1981): 216–30. Examines the centrality of night imagery as a mysterious symbol throughout Chopin's fiction.

———. "Techniques of Distancing in the Fiction of Kate Chopin." *Southern Studies* 24, no. 1 (Spring 1985): 69–81. Examines Chopin's artistically devious methods of introducing sexual content.

Eble, Kenneth. "A Forgotten Novel: Kate Chopin's *The Awakening.*" *Western Humanities Review* 10, no. 3 (Summer 1956): 261–69. Discovers *The Awakening* for the American public.

Fletcher, Marie. "The Southern Woman in the Fiction of Kate Chopin." *Louisiana History* 7 (Spring 1966): 117–32. Discusses Chopin as a writer who begins to challenge the traditional concept of southern womanhood.

Fox-Genovese, Elizabeth. "Kate Chopin's *Awakening.*" *Southern Studies* 18 (Fall 1979): 261–90. Suggests that although Edna's behavior reflects a strong critique of patriarchal society, Edna ultimately fails because her need for a mother causes her to regress.

Franklin, Rosemary F. "*The Awakening* and the Failure of Psyche." *American Literature* 56, no. 4 (December 1984): 510–26. Compares Edna and the mythic Psyche to illustrate Edna's complex struggle.

Gilbert, Sandra M. "The Second Coming of Aphrodite: Kate Chopin's Fantasy of Desire." *Kenyon Review*, n.s. 5 (Summer 1983): 42–66. Discusses *The Awakening* as a fantasy of nineteenth-century Aphroditian rebirth.

Selected Bibliography

Justus, James H. "The Unawakening of Edna Pontellier." *Southern Literary Journal* 10 (Spring 1978): 107–22. Asserts that Edna achieves only partial self-knowledge.

Kauffmann, Stanley. "The Really Lost Generation." *New Republic* 155 (3 December 1966): 22, 37–38. Praises *The Awakening* for its modern existential voice—and mourns its neglect.

Kearns, Katherine. "The Nullification of Edna Pontellier." *American Literature* 63, no. 1 (March 1991): 62–88. Sees Edna as nullified by her masculine definition of selfhood.

Koloski, Bernard. "Notes: The Swinburne Lines in *The Awakening*." *American Literature* 45 (January 1974): 608–10. Suggests that the Swinburne lines forecast Edna's suicide.

Lant, Kathleen Margaret. "The Siren of Grand Isle: Adèle's Role in *The Awakening*." *Southern Studies* 23, no. 2 (Summer 1984): 167–75. Discusses Adèle as a siren figure who both lures Edna and endangers her.

Lattin, Patricia Hopkins. "Childbirth and Motherhood in Kate Chopin's Fiction." *Regionalism and the Female Imagination* 4 (Spring 1978): 8–12. Suggests that motherhood has disastrous consequences for Chopin's women.

———. "The Search for Self in Kate Chopin's Fiction: Simple Versus Complex Vision." *Southern Studies* 21, no. 2 (1982): 222–35. Discusses Chopin's modern refusal to see the achievement of selfhood as easy, or even possible.

Leary, Lewis. "Kate Chopin, Liberationist?" *Southern Literary Journal* 3 (Fall 1970): 138–44. Reacts to Seyersted's two major 1969 publications, concluding that Chopin was not crusading for women's rights but arguing for spiritual freedom.

———. "Kate Chopin and Walt Whitman." *Walt Whitman Review* 16 (December 1970): 120–21. Discusses Whitman's influence on *The Awakening*.

Leder, Priscilla. "An American Dilemma: Cultural Conflict in Kate Chopin's *The Awakening*." *Southern Studies* 22, no. 1 (1983): 97–104. Compares the attraction to "natural" cultures in *The Awakening* and *Typee*.

May, John R. "Local Color in *The Awakening*." *Southern Review* 6 (Autumn 1970): 1031–40. Suggests that local color detail in *The Awakening* is integral to the unfolding of Edna's sexuality.

Mitsutani, Margaret. "Kate Chopin's *The Awakening*: The Narcissism of Edna Pontellier." *Studies in English Literature* (1986): 3–15. Discusses Edna's narcissism as an attempt to escape society and return to the self.

Ringe, Donald A. "Romantic Imagery in Kate Chopin's *The Awakening*." *American Literature* 43 (January 1972): 580–88. Discusses Chopin's elaborate use of romantic imagery.

Rocks, James E. "Kate Chopin's Ironic Vision." *Revue de Louisiane/Louisiana Review* 1 (Winter 1972): 110–20. Concludes that Chopin is an ironist fascinated by multiple truths.

Rosen, Kenneth M. "Kate Chopin's *The Awakening*: Ambiguity as Art." *Journal of American Studies* 5 (August 1971): 197–99. Sees *The Awakening* as a novel that raises questions but resists answers.

Rosowski, Susan J. "The Novel of Awakening." *Genre* 12, no. 3 (Fall 1979): 313–32. Examines works by Gustave Flaubert, Kate Chopin, Willa Cather, Agnes Smedley, and George Eliot as novels of "awakening."

Skaggs, Peggy. "Three Tragic Figures in Kate Chopin's *The Awakening*." *Louisiana Studies* 13 (Winter 1974): 345–64. Discusses Edna Pontellier as an even more tragic figure than Adèle Ratignolle or Mademoiselle Reisz.

Spangler, George. "Kate Chopin's *The Awakening*: A Partial Dissent." *Novel: A Forum on Fiction* 3 (Spring 1970): 249–55. Analyzes Edna's despair as a result of disappointed love.

Sullivan, Ruth, and Stewart Smith. "Narrative Stance in Kate Chopin's *The Awakening*." *Studies in American Fiction* 1 (Spring 1973): 62–75. Believes that contradictory views of Edna are advanced through Chopin's narrative technique.

Thornton, Lawrence. "*The Awakening*: A Political Romance." *American Literature* 52, no. 1 (March 1980): 50–66. Focuses on the irresolvable conflict between Edna's aspirations and strict Creole conventions.

Toth, Emily. "Kate Chopin on Divine Love and Suicide: Two Rediscovered Articles." *American Literature* 63, no. 1 (March 1991): 115–21. Discloses the contents of two 1899 newspaper articles about love and suicide.

———. "Kate Chopin's *The Awakening* as Feminist Criticism." *Louisiana Studies* 15 (Fall 1976): 241–51. Shows how *The Awakening* translates feminist theory into fiction.

Urgo, Joseph R. "A Prologue to Rebellion: *The Awakening* and the Habit of Self-Expression." *Southern Literary Journal* 20, no. 1 (Fall 1987): 22–32. Sees Edna's awakening as a preface to rebellion.

Walker, Nancy. "Feminist or Naturalist: The Social Context of Kate Chopin's *The Awakening*." *Southern Quarterly* 17, no. 2 (1979): 95–103. Argues that Chopin did not intend *The Awakening* to be a feminist tract.

Wheeler, Otis B. "The Five Awakenings of Edna Pontellier." *Southern Review* 11 (January 1975): 118–28. Discusses the progressive stages of Edna's awakening, concluding with her existential despair.

Selected Bibliography

Wolff, Cynthia Griffin. "Thanatos and Eros: Kate Chopin's *The Awakening*." *American Quarterly* 25 (October 1973): 449–71. Argues that Edna's disintegration is due to oral fixation and the dream of complete fulfillment—not to the victimization by society.

Wymard, Eleanor B. "Kate Chopin: Her Existential Imagination." *Southern Studies* 19, no. 4 (Winter 1980): 373–84. Discusses Chopin's similarities to existentialists like Jean-Paul Sartre, Albert Camus, and Paul Tillich.

Yaeger, Patricia S. "'A Language Which Nobody Understood': Emancipatory Strategies in *The Awakening*." *Novel: A Forum on Fiction* 20, no. 3 (Spring 1987): 197–219. Argues that Edna's most transgressive act is her attempt to free herself from normative male language.

Zlotnick, Joan. "A Woman's Will: Kate Chopin on Selfhood, Wifehood, and Motherhood." *Markham Review* 3 (October 1968): 1–5. Proposes that, like D. H. Lawrence, Chopin frequently examines marital discord in her fiction through poetry and psychological argument.

Bibliographies

Bonner, Thomas, Jr. "Kate Chopin: An Annotated Bibliography." *Bulletin of Bibliography* 32 (July-September 1975): 101–5.

Inge, Tonette Bond. "Kate Chopin." In *American Women Writers: Bibliographical Essays*, edited by Maurice Duke, Jackson R. Bryer, and M. Thomas Inge, 47–69. Westport, Conn.: Greenwood Press, 1983.

Potter, Richard H. "Kate Chopin and Her Critics: An Annotated Checklist." *Missouri Historical Society Bulletin* 26 (1970): 306–17.

Seyersted, Per. "Kate Chopin (1851–1904)." *American Literary Realism* 3 (Spring 1970), 153–59.

Springer, Marlene. *Edith Wharton and Kate Chopin: A Reference Guide.* Boston: G. K. Hall & Co., 1976.

———. "Kate Chopin: A Reference Guide Updated." *Resources for American Literary Study* 11 (Autumn 1981): 280–303.

Toth, Emily. "Bibliography of Writings on Kate Chopin." In *A Kate Chopin Miscellany*, edited by Per Seyersted and Emily Toth, 212–61. Natchitoches, La.: Northwestern State University Press, 1979.

Index

Index

Fryer, Judith, 115
Fuller, Henry B: *With the Procession*, 43
Fuller, Margaret, 105

gender roles, 41, 103
Gilbert, Sandra, 27, 66, 89, 114, 123n31
Gilder, R.W., 8–9, 33
Gilman, Charlotte Perkins: *Women and Economics*, 6, 9, 10, 15, 50, 55
Gilmore, Michael, 26, 27, 36, 62, 90
Giorcelli, Cristina, 28, 51, 56, 112, 126n2
Glasgow, Ellen, 6
Goldman, Dorothy, 108–09
Goreau, Angeline, 116
Grand Isle, 46, 54–59, 64
Grand Isle (film), 29, 36
Greer, Germaine: *The Obstacle Race*, 88, 90

Hearn, Lafcadio: *Chita*, 28, 59–60
Hoder-Salmon, Marilyn, 25
Howells, William Dean: *Criticism and Fiction*, 9; *Modern Instance*, 8; *The Rise of Silas Lapham*, 44, 67
Huf, Linda, 26, 46

Ibsen, Henrik, 125n4; *Hedda Gabler*, 45
imitation, 36–38, 114
Inheritance, 15, 52
irony, 44, 49, 60, 78, 81, 110; of title, 96

James, Henry, 29, 45–46
Jewett, Sarah Orne, 6
Jones, Mary Harris, 7
Justus, James, 26
Kate Chopin Newsletter, 24

Kauffman, Stanley, 22
Kelley, Mary, 75, 88
Kittredge, Charmian, 5
Klondike, 5, 45
Koloski, Bernard, 17, 23, 24, 70
Koudis, Virginia, 115
Krantz Hotel, 54

Lafitte, Jean, 77–78
language, 36
Lattin, Patricia Hopkins, 27, 89, 98, 106
Leary, Lewis, 22, 23, 24
London, Jack, 5, 127n9
Lupton, Mary Jane, 130n2

marriage, 6, 7–8; and Napoleonic Code, 10–11
Martin, Wendy, 24, 34, 116
Maupassant, Guy de, 33
medicine, practice of, 10
Melville, Herman: *Moby-Dick*, 110; *Typee*, 28
Mitsutani, Margaret, 116
Moers, Ellen: *Literary Women*, 35
money, 50–52
"Mother Jones." *See* Jones, Mary Harris
motherhood, 17, 27, 35, 41, 61, 100–6; absence of in women artist/writers, 105–6, symbols of, 60–61
Mott, Lucretia, 6
Murfree, Mary Noailles, 20; *The Prophet of the Great Smoky Mountains*, 8
myths: of the Fisher King, 78–79; Greek, 56–61, 64, 68, 72–73, 80, 112; of Sleeping Beauty, 62–63, 80

Neuls-Bates, Carol: *Women in Music*, 87

Index

The Author

Joyce Dyer is assistant professor of English and director of writing at Hiram College in Hiram, Ohio. In 1990–91 she was Ohio's recipient of the Teacher-Scholar Award, funded by the National Endowment for the Humanities and Reader's Digest. Dyer, the author of numerous essays and articles, has a special interest in southern literature and Appalachian studies. Her essays on Chopin have been included in Harold Bloom's Modern Critical Views edition of *Kate Chopin* (1987) and in (the MLA volume) *Approaches to Teaching Chopin's "The Awakening"* (1988).

Explain the way Awake, wo, & Gatsby all represent 2 worlds, stand perched between 2 worlds